SETTING THE RECORD STRAIGHT
EMMA SMITH:
AN ELECT LADY

Cover: The images on the cover represent Joseph and Emma Smith.

SETTING THE RECORD STRAIGHT

EMMA SMITH: AN ELECT LADY

Susan Easton Black

Millennial Press, Inc.
P.O. Box 1741
Orem, UT 84059

ISBN: 1-932597-52-2

Cover design and typesetting by Adam Riggs

Dedication

To Melva Hahl for keeping Emma's tradition of charity alive in Nauvoo.

Contents

Acknowledgments

Providing answers to the questions asked in this text would not have been possible without access to significant resources in archives and libraries. I am very appreciative of the staff at the Church History Library in Salt Lake City and at the L. Tom Perry Special Collections at Brigham Young University. The same courteous assistance was given by research assistant Audrey Gonzalez, editor Heather Seferovich, and colleagues at BYU. To each of them, I express gratitude and admiration for their many talents so willingly shared.

Introduction

Emma Hale Smith Bidamon is arguably the most famous woman in nineteenth-century Latter-day Saint history. Much has been spoken and written about her life—some has been positive and some negative. Unfortunately, Emma's existing writings do not clarify her polarizing role in Mormonism. The topic of her life has left more than one presenter frustrated because Emma did not keep a journal, write an autobiography, or pen short vignettes of special events in her life. Such omissions leave biographers looking to the collected works of those who knew her best.

Oil portrait, artist unknown, ca. 1842.

A primary source has been the journal entries of her husband Joseph Smith. While these provide factual information, there is little commentary in them. Examples include "Continued translating and revising, and reading letters in the evening, Sister Emma being present in the office";[1] "In the afternoon rode to Brother John Benbows, on horseback, accompanied by Emma and others";[2] "Walked to the store with Emma";[3]

"Rode to the big mound on the LaHarpe road, accompanied by Emma";[4] and "Spent the forenoon chiefly in conversation with Emma on various subjects, and in reading history with her—both felt in good spirits and very cheerful."[5] Other family members and friends also recorded information about Emma. Her children's and grandchildren's writings provide only glimpses into her life, such as, "Every body knew of Mother Bidamon's salves for cuts—bruises—fever—rheumatism—for every kind of ache & pain,"[6] and journalist Emmeline B. Wells penned, "[Emma] was a queen in her home, so to speak, and beloved by the people, who were many of them indebted to her for favors and kindnesses."[7]

But the question remains, "Who was Emma Smith?" Unable to dismiss the question, some biographers place Emma in settings that are not always supported by historical evidence. They tell of feelings that may or may not have been hers when discussing sacred doctrines and her relationship with her husband. These writers use words such as *perhaps* or *maybe* or phrases like *one can imagine* to try to interpret Emma's life. Their conclusions may or may not be correct.

Emma Smith: an Elect Lady is written in hopes of setting the record straight. The author believes that the life of Emma, the wife of a prophet of God, deserves to be presented through reliable sources. It is hoped that readers will appreciate a documented approach to the life of this extraordinary woman.

Chronology of Emma Hale Smith Bidamon

1804

July 10   Emma Hale, daughter of Isaac Hale and Eliza-
                 beth Lewis, is born in Harmony, Susquehanna
                 County, Pennsylvania.

1804–1825

Emma grows to maturity in Harmony.

1825

October–   Josiah Stowell hires Joseph Smith Jr. to dig for
November   Spanish treasure in Harmony; Joseph meets
                 Emma Hale.

1827

January 18   Joseph and Emma are married by Zachariah
                 Tarble, a justice of the peace, in South Bain-
                 bridge, New York.

                 Joseph and Emma live with Joseph Sr. and
                 Lucy Mack Smith in Palmyra, New York.

September 22   Emma is the first to learn that Joseph has ob-
                 tained the Book of Mormon plates from the
                 angel Moroni.

1828

Joseph and Emma become residents of Harmony.

June 15 Emma gives birth to Alvin Smith; baby Alvin dies.

Emma is a scribe for Joseph as he translates the Book of Mormon.

1830

April 6 The Church of Christ (later known as The Church of Jesus Christ of Latter-day Saints) is organized in Fayette, New York.

June 28 Emma is baptized a member of the Church of Christ by Oliver Cowdery.

July Emma is the subject of a revelation from God given to Joseph (D&C 25).

September–October Emma sews clothing for the missionaries called to journey to the "borders of the Lamanites" (D&C 28, 30–32).

1831

February 1 Joseph and Emma arrive in Kirtland, Ohio.

April 30 Emma gives birth to twins, Louisa and Thaddeus; the twins die.

May Emma becomes the adoptive mother of twins—Joseph and Julia Murdock.

September 11 Joseph and Emma and the Murdock twins begin residing in Hiram, Ohio.

1832

March 29   Joseph Smith Murdock dies from complications of measles and a cold at age eleven months.

May 1   William W. Phelps is called to "correct and print the Hymns which had been selected by Emma Smith, in fulfillment of the revelation" (see D&C 25).

June 6   Joseph writes to Emma from Greenville, Indiana: "I am happy to find that you are still in the faith of Christ."

September 12 Joseph and Emma and their children reside at the Gilbert & Whitney Store in Kirtland.

October 13   Joseph writes to Emma from New York City: "Thoughts of home of Emma and Julia rushes upon my mind like a flood."

November 6   Emma gives birth to Joseph Smith III in an upper room of the Gilbert & Whitney Store.

1833

February 27 Joseph receives a revelation known as the "Word of Wisdom" (D&C 89), in part, because of Emma's concern over tobacco use, which led Joseph to inquire of the Lord.

March 6   Joseph writes to Emma about the need to "commit the cross plow unto the hands of the poor."

1834

May 19   Joseph writes to Emma from Richmond, Indiana: "I pray God to let his blessings to rest upon you and the children."

June 4   Joseph writes to Emma from the banks of the Mississippi River: "We all enjoy the fruits of our labour if we hold out faithful to the end which I pray may be the happy lot of us all."

December 9   Joseph Smith Sr. gives Emma a patriarchal blessing; Oliver Cowdery is the scribe.

1835

September 14   Emma is assigned "to make a selection of Sacred Hymns, and W. W. Phelps appointed to revise and arrange them for printing."

1836

A Collection of Sacred Hymns for the Church of the Latter Day Saints is published.

March 27   Joseph petitions the Lord, "Have mercy, O Lord, upon [my] wife and children, that they may be exalted in thy presence, and preserved by thy fostering hand" (D&C 109:69).

June 20   Emma gives birth to Frederick Granger Williams Smith in Kirtland.

August 19   Joseph writes to Emma from Salem, Massachusetts: "You may know that you and the children are much on my mind."

1838

January 12   Joseph leaves Kirtland to escape mob violence; Emma travels to Far West, Missouri.

June 2   Emma gives birth to Alexander Hale Smith in Far West.

November 4	Joseph writes to Emma from Independence, Missouri: "I would inform you that I am well, and that we are all of us in good spirits as regards our own fate."
November 12	Joseph writes to Emma from Richmond, Missouri: "I received your letter which I read over and over again, it was a sweet morsal to me."
December 1	Joseph writes to Emma from Liberty, Missouri: "We arrived in Liberty and [were] committed to jail this evening but we are all in good spirits."
December	Emma visits Joseph in Liberty Jail.

1839

February 15	Emma and her children leave Missouri by crossing the Mississippi River to reach Quincy, Illinois.
March 7	Emma writes to Joseph from Quincy: "No one but God, knows the reflections of my mind and the feelings of my heart when I left our house and home, and allmost all of every thing that we possessed excepting our little children, and took my journey out of the State of Missouri."
March 21	Joseph writes to Emma from Liberty Jail: "I want to be with you very much but the powers of mobocracy is too many at present."
April 4	Joseph writes to Emma from Liberty Jail: "I would gladly go from here to you barefoot, and bareheaded, and half naked, to see you and think it great pleasure."

April 22	Joseph joins Emma in Quincy after escaping from his captors in Missouri.
May 10	Joseph and Emma and their children move to Commerce (later known as Nauvoo), Illinois.
Summer	Joseph and Emma care for the sick of Commerce; their home provides shelter for the incapacitated.
October 27	The high council of Nauvoo votes that "Sister Emma Smith select and publish a hymn-book for the use of the Church."
November 9	Joseph writes to Emma from Springfield, Illinois: "Believe me feelings are of the best kind towards you."

1840

January 20	Joseph writes to Emma from Philadelphia, Pennsylvania: "The time seems long that I am deprived of your society."
June 13	Emma gives birth to Don Carlos Smith in Nauvoo.
November 1	The *Times and Seasons* announces that Emma will compile another hymnal.

1841

Emma compiles a hymnal, consisting of 304 hymns.

May 15	Emma becomes a property owner in Nauvoo.

1842

Emma gives birth to an unnamed son in Nauvoo.

March 17	Emma is elected president of the Female Relief Society of Nauvoo.
August 16	Joseph writes to Emma while in hiding: "Tongue cannot express the gratitude of my heart, for the warm and true-hearted friendship you have manifested."
August 17	Emma writes to Governor Thomas Carlin of Illinois: "May I entreat your Excellency to lighten the hand of oppression and persecution which is laid upon me and my family."
August 27	Emma writes to Governor Thomas Carlin of Illinois: "I entreat your honor . . . [to stop] persecution that you are well aware, is entirely without any just foundation or excuse."

1843

Emma is baptized by proxy for her father Isaac Hale, her mother Elizabeth Hale, and other family members (Phebe Roote, Eunice Ward Cady, and Reuben Hale).

July 12	Joseph records a revelation on the new and everlasting covenant of marriage (D&C 132); Emma rejects the revelation.
August 31	Joseph and Emma and their children move into the Mansion House in Nauvoo.

1844

June 23	Joseph writes to Emma from Iowa: "May God Almighty bless you & the children & Mother & all my friends."

June 25	Joseph writes to Emma from Carthage, Illinois: "Myself & Hyrum have been again arrested for Treason."
June 27	Joseph writes to Emma; "I am very much resigned to my lot knowing I am justified and have done the best that could be done give my love to the children and all my friends."
	A mob kills Joseph and his brother Hyrum Smith in Carthage.
November 17	Emma gives birth to David Hyrum Smith in Nauvoo.

1845

December 9	The New York *Sun* prints a November 20, 1845, letter signed by Emma Smith; Emma renounces the letter as a forgery; her denial is printed in the *Times and Seasons* on January 15, 1846.

1846

September 10–11	Fire damages the Mansion House during the Battle of Nauvoo.
September 12	Emma and her children take passage on the steamer *Uncle Toby* to Fulton, Illinois; in Fulton, Emma rents a house.

1847

February	Emma and her children return to Nauvoo; Emma opens the Mansion House as a hotel.

December 23 Emma marries Lewis Crum Bidamon; Reverend William Haney, a Methodist minister, performs the service.

1849

Lewis Bidamon journeys to the gold fields of California; Emma remains in Nauvoo.

September 10 John Bernhisel writes to Brigham Young: "Though Emma received me in the kindest, and entertained me in the most hospitable manner, yet she did not make a single inquiry in relation to the valley, the Church, or any of its members."

1850

January 7 Emma writes to Lewis Bidamon from Nauvoo: "I have scarcely enjoyed any good thing since you left home."

Summer Lewis Bidamon leaves California and returns to Nauvoo.

1851

Emma cares for Lucy Mack Smith, Joseph's mother, in the Mansion House; Lucy dies on May 14, 1856, at age eighty-one.

1853

Frederick Piercy, an artist, visits Nauvoo and reports, "I found the whole family [Emma's family] had obtained a most excellent reputation for integrity and industry."

1856

October 30   Emma is visited by George A. Smith and Erastus Snow, members of the Quorum of the Twelve Apostles, from Salt Lake Valley.

1860

April 6   Emma is welcomed as a member of the Reorganized Church of Jesus Christ of Latter Day Saints (RLDS).

June 28   Emma is visited by her nephew Joseph F. Smith and relative Samuel H. B. Smith; Joseph F. recalls, "[Emma] said she would have known me anywhere because I looked so much like father!!"

1861

Emma compiles *Latter Day Saints' Selection of Hymns* for the RLDS Church.

1868

Emma accepts care of four-year-old Charles Edwin Bidamon, son of Lewis Bidamon and Nancy Abercrombie.

1871

Emma moves from the Mansion House to a brick house, known as the Riverside Mansion or Bidamon House, near the Mississippi River in Nauvoo.

1872

Emma falls down the cellar steps in the Mansion House; fractures her left arm.

1879

February 4–10 Emma is interviewed by her son Joseph Smith III; the interview is printed in the *Saints' Herald* on October 1, 1879.

April 30 Emma dies in Nauvoo at age seventy-four.

May 2 Emma is buried next to Joseph Smith Jr. in the Smith family graveyard in Nauvoo.

Emma Hale
Smith Bidamon
Q&A

Where was Emma reared?

Emma, the third daughter and seventh child of Isaac Hale and Elizabeth Lewis, was born on July 10, 1804, in Harmony, Susquehanna County, Pennsylvania. She grew to maturity in Harmony's rural surroundings in "a comfortable home (foundation dimensions are thirty by forty-two feet)."[8]

In that home, she met young Joseph Smith Jr. At the time of their meeting, Emma was twenty-two years old, stood about five feet nine inches tall, had dark hair and brown eyes, and was described as having "excellent form . . . [and] splendid physical developments."[9]

What type of work was Joseph Smith doing at the time he met Emma Hale?

In the 1820s respected citizens and greedy speculators alike believed that great treasures, even a legendary lost Spanish silver mine, were concealed in the northeast section of the United States. Men scoured the land looking for hidden wealth. With this backdrop, and "on account of having heard that [Joseph] possessed certain keys, by which he could discern things invisible to the natural eye," Joseph was hired to dig for a lost silver mine in the Oquago Mountain at Harmony, Pennsylvania. Although he "endeavored to divert [his employer] from the vain pursuit," Joseph accepted the terms of employment and

in October 1825 went to Harmony to commence digging.[10]
It was this move to Harmony that brought Emma in contact
with Joseph.

"I continued to work for nearly a month, without success
in [my] undertaking, and finally I prevailed with the old gen-
tleman to cease digging after it," wrote Joseph.[11] The digging
stopped on November 17, 1825, about one month after it had
begun.

How did Isaac Hale, Emma's father, react to Joseph Smith?

According to Lucy Mack Smith, Joseph "immediately commenced paying his addresses" to Emma Hale after his arrival
in Harmony.[12] Such attention was not pleasing to her father. "I
first became acquainted with Joseph Smith, Jr., in November,
1825," wrote Isaac. "He was at that time in the employ of a set
of men who were called 'money-diggers,' and his occupation
was that of seeing, or pretending to see, by means of a stone
placed in his hat, and his hat closed over his face. In this way
he pretended to discover minerals and hidden treasure."[13]

Joseph attributed the animosity of Emma's father to "my
continuing to assert that I had seen a vision."[14]

Isaac recalled that Joseph "made several visits at my house,
and at length asked my consent to his marrying my daughter
Emma. This I refused."[15] His refusal did not stop Joseph from
seeking Emma's favor or asking Joseph Knight to furnish him
"with a horse and cutter [sled] to go and see his girl."[16]

When Joseph returned to Palmyra, he often thought of
Emma. Mother Smith wrote that Joseph "thought that no
young woman that he ever was acquainted with was better
calculated to render the man of her choice happy than Miss
Emma Hale, a young lady, whom he had been extremely fond
of since his first introduction to her."[17] According to Mother

Smith, Joseph remarked, "I have been very lonely ever since Alvin [his brother] died, and I have concluded to get married; and if you have no objections to uniting myself in marriage with Miss Emma Hale, she would be my choice in preference to any other woman I have ever seen."[18]

Did Joseph marry Emma without the approval of her father?

Emma was married to Joseph on January 18, 1827, in South Bainbridge, New York, by Squire Tarbell [Tarble]. "I had no intention of marrying when I left home," Emma wrote, "but . . . [Joseph] urged me to marry him, and preferring to marry him to any other man I knew, I consented."[19] At the time, Joseph was twenty-one years old and Emma twenty-two, so both were old enough to make this decision legally. (She was seventeen months older than him.)

Upon learning of Emma's marriage to Joseph, Isaac Hale lamented, "You have stolen my daughter and married her. I had much rather have followed her to her grave."[20]

Did Joseph Smith's parents welcome the newlyweds into the family home in Palmyra?

"Immediately after my marriage," wrote Joseph Smith, "[Emma and I] went to my father's, and farmed with him that season."[21]

When Joseph and Emma arrived at his parents' farmhouse, Mother Smith recalled, "I anticipated as much happiness with my second daughter-in-law, as I had received great pleasure from the society of the first."[22]

Lucy Mack Smith, mother-in-law of Emma Smith Bidamon

Lucy Mack Smith recognized in Emma an unselfish desire to serve others:

Whatever her hands found to do she did with her might, until so far beyond her strength that she brought upon herself a heavy fit of sickness, which lasted four weeks. And although her strength was exhausted, still her spirits were the same, which, in fact, was always the case with her, even under the most trying circumstances. I have never seen a woman in my life who would endure every species of fatigue and hardship from month to month and from year to year with that unflinching courage, zeal, and patience which she has ever done; for I know that which she has had to endure—she has been tossed upon the ocean of uncertainty—she has breasted the storms of persecution, and buffeted the rage of men and devils, which would have borne down almost any other woman.[23]

Was Emma the first to learn that Joseph had received the gold plates from the angel Moroni?

Near midnight on September 22, 1827, Emma waited in the buggy while Joseph climbed the Hill Cumorah to converse with the angel Moroni. Of that event, Joseph penned,

the same heavenly messenger delivered [the plates] up to me with this charge: that I should be responsible for them; that if I should let them go carelessly, or through any neglect of mine, I should be cut off; but that if I would use all my endeavors to preserve them, until he, the messenger, should call for them, they should be protected.[24]

When Joseph returned to the buggy with plates in hand, Emma was the first to learn that he had received the gold plates from the angel Moroni.

What caused Joseph and Emma to leave Palmyra, New York, and journey to Harmony, Pennsylvania?

As word of Joseph's acquisition of the gold plates spread, curiosity, harassment, and persecution followed. Assailants tried to take what they called Joe's "Gold Bible." Cash and property were offered for a glimpse of the plates. When Joseph refused to show the plates to anyone, schemes were contrived to snatch the treasure. Keeping the plates safe proved difficult for Joseph. A birch log, hearth stones, floor boards, flax, and a barrel of beans were used to keep thieves at bay, but there was little stopping mobocracy from mushrooming in Palmyra.

As frenzy over the "Gold Bible" mounted, Joseph was "under the necessity of leaving" the Palmyra area. He turned to Isaac Hale in Harmony, asking for refuge from the mob element in Palmyra. Isaac agreed to house Joseph and Emma. He welcomed his daughter and son-in-law into his home in winter 1827, and there Joseph "commenced copying the characters off the plates."[25]

What caused Joseph and Emma to abruptly leave the Isaac Hale farmhouse?

When Isaac discovered that Joseph had a chest containing secret contents (the gold plates), hospitality ended. Isaac "was determined to see" the plates.[26] Joseph refused. "After this I became dissatisfied, and informed him that if there was anything in my house of that description, which I could not be allowed to see, he must take it away," said Father Hale.[27] His stance and Joseph's refusal led to a family rift that was slow to mend. Joseph and Emma, feeling unwelcome in the Hale farmhouse, left. They did not move far away, however. The couple took up residence in a small dwelling in Harmony near Isaac's home.

Did Emma see the gold plates while they were in Joseph's possession?

In their small home in Harmony, the plates "lay in a box under our bed for months," recalled Emma, "but I never felt at liberty to look at them."[28] They "often lay on the table without any attempt at concealment, wrapped in a small linen table cloth, which I had given him to fold them in. I once felt of the plates, as they thus lay on the table, tracing their outline and shape." To Emma, the plates "seemed to be pliable like thick paper, and would rustle with a metallic sound when the edges were moved by the thumb, as one does sometimes thumb the edges of a book."[29]

Was the birth of her first child difficult for Emma?

On June 15, 1828, Emma gave birth to a son named Alvin. Unfortunately, Alvin died within hours of his birth. After his death, Emma "seemed to tremble upon the verge of the silent home of her infant. So uncertain seemed her fate for a season that, in the space of two weeks, Joseph never slept one hour in undisturbed quiet."[30]

Did Emma serve as a scribe for the Book of Mormon translation?

Joseph explained, "I have again commenced translating [Book of Mormon], and Emma writes for me, but the angel said that the Lord would send me a scribe, and I trust that it will be so."[31] Lucy Mack Smith explained why Emma did not record more than a few pages of the translation: "Emma had so much of her time taken up with the care of her house that she could write but little for him."[32]

Of the Book of Mormon translation, Emma said:

> My belief is that the Book of Mormon is of divine authenticity—I have not the slightest doubt of

it. I am satisfied that no man could have dictated the writing of the manuscripts unless he was inspired; for, when acting as his scribe, your father [this was said to Joseph Smith III] would dictate to me hour after hour; and when returning after meals, or after interruptions, he would at once begin where he had left off, without either seeing the manuscript or having any portion of it read to him. This was a usual thing for him to do. It would have been improbable that a learned man could do this; and, for one so ignorant and unlearned as he was, it was simply impossible.[33]

The main scribe of the Book of Mormon was Oliver Cowdery, who testified, "I wrote with my own pen the entire Book of Mormon (save a few pages) as it fell from the lips of the Prophet, as he translated it by the gift and power of God, by means of the Urim and Thummim. . . . That book is true."[34]

Did Joseph discuss with Emma any portion of the Book of Mormon translation?

In winter 1856, Emma recalled that as Joseph was translating he "could not pronounce the word Sariah." He asked, "Emma, did Jerusalem have walls surrounding it?" "When I informed him that it had," said Emma, Joseph replied, "O, I thought I was deceived."[35]

Did a disagreement with Emma cause Joseph to loose the ability to translate the Book of Mormon?

David Whitmer remembered one morning as Joseph was preparing to translate passages from the gold plates:

Something went wrong about the house and he was put out about it. Something that Emma, his wife, had done. Oliver and I went up stairs, and Joseph came up soon after to continue the translation, but he could not do anything. He could not translate a single syllable. He went down stairs, out into the orchard and made supplication to the Lord; was gone about an hour—came back to the house, and asked Emma's forgiveness and then came up stairs where we were and the translation went on all right.[36]

Was Emma baptized the day the Church of Christ [later known as The Church of Jesus Christ of Latter-day Saints] was organized?

Emma's testimony of the Book of Mormon and the prophetic calling of her husband led to her baptism on June 28, 1830, by Oliver Cowdery. According to Joseph, Emma's willingness to submit to baptism and the willingness of others to submit to that ordinance was "a sign to God, to angels, and to heaven that we do the will of God, and there is no other way beneath the heavens whereby God hath ordained for man to come to Him to be saved, and enter into the kingdom of God, except faith in Jesus Christ, repentance, and baptism for the remission of sins, and any other course is in vain."[37]

Was it soon after Emma's baptism that Joseph received a revelation from God for her?

In July 1830, soon after her baptism, Joseph received an important revelation for Emma. The revelation is found in Doctrine and Covenants 25 and begins, "Hearken unto the voice of the Lord your God, while I speak unto you, Emma Smith, my daughter." In the revelation, Emma was told, "Behold, thy sins are forgiven thee, and thou art an elect lady, whom I have called" (D&C 25:3). The word *elect* was defined by Joseph on March 17, 1842, when he told the women of the newly formed Female Relief Society of Nauvoo that "elect meant to be elected to a certain work, &c., and that the revelation was then fulfilled by Sister Emma's election to the Presidency of the Society."[38]

What was the calling given to Emma by God?

Her calling was to be the wife of a prophet of God. In this role, Emma was told, "the office of thy calling shall be for a comfort unto my servant, Joseph Smith, Jun., thy husband." She was to use "consoling words, in the spirit of meekness" with him. She was to cleave to Joseph and to "go with him at the time of his going, and be unto him for a scribe." She was promised that for faithfully fulfilling her calling, her "husband shall support thee in the church" (D&C 25:5, 6, 9).

Emmeline B. Wells wrote about Emma fulfilling her calling as Joseph Smith's wife:

> Emma was a great solace to her husband in all his persecutions and the severe ordeals through which he passed; she was always ready to encourage and comfort him, devoted to his interests, and was constantly by him whenever it was possible. She was a queen in her home, so to speak, and beloved by the people, who were many of them indebted to her for favors and kindnesses.[39]

Emma exemplified Joseph's teaching:

> Teach women how to behave towards their husbands, to treat them with mildness and affection. When a man is borne down with trouble, when he is perplexed with care and difficulty, if he can meet a smile instead of an argument or a murmur—if he can meet with mildness, it will calm down his soul

and soothe his feelings; when the mind is going to despair, it needs a solace of affection and kindness. When you go home, never give a cross or unkind word to your husbands, but let kindness, charity and love crown your works henceforward.[40]

Was it by revelation that Emma was appointed to select hymns for the Church?

Emma compiled the first LDS hymnal.

By revelation, Emma was told to expound scriptures, exhort the Church, and write, learn and select sacred hymns (D&C 25:7, 8, 11). At a meeting of the Kirtland High Council and Presidency of the Church held on September 14, 1835—the very same meeting in which Joseph Smith Sr. was called to pronounce patriarchal blessings and Oliver Cowdery to be a Church recorder—"it was further decided that Sister Emma Smith proceed to make a selection of Sacred Hymns, according to the revelation; and that President W. W. Phelps be appointed to revise and arrange them for printing."[41] Emma fulfilled the assignment. She compiled a pocket-sized hymnal titled *A Collection of Sacred Hymns for the Church of the Latter Day Saints.* The hymnal contained ninety hymns, the first being "Know This That Every Soul Is Free." Thirty-four of the selected hymns were authored by Church members; twenty-six of those were contributed by William W. Phelps.[42]

Was Emma a gifted musician?

Emma's gift for music was singing. "I arrived at [Joseph's] house about nine o'clock, just as his family was singing, before the accustomed evening prayer," penned William Holmes Walker. "[Joseph's] wife Emma, leading in the singing. I thought I had never heard such a sweet, heavenly music before."[43]

Is it evident that Joseph prayed to the Lord in behalf of his wife Emma?

Joseph pleaded with the Lord on Emma's behalf and the behalf of their children: "Have mercy, O Lord, upon [my] wife and children, that they may be exalted in thy presence, and preserved by thy fostering hand" (D&C 109:69). In answer to his plea, Emma again became the subject of a revelation. In Doctrine and Covenants 132, she was told to "abide and cleave unto my servant Joseph, and to none else." She was admonished to "forgive my servant Joseph his trespasses; and then shall she be forgiven her trespasses, . . . and I, the Lord thy God, will bless her, and multiply her, and make her heart to rejoice" (D&C 132:54, 56).

Did Emma receive warnings by way of revelation?

Emma was warned in a revelation that despite her position as an "elect lady" and the wife of a prophet, she must endure faithfully to the end or risk losing all, for unless she did endure, "where I am you cannot come" (D&C 25:15). The Lord also warned that he would "destroy her if she abide not in my law" (D&C 132:54). Elder Bruce R. McConkie wrote, "Just as it is possible for the very elect to be deceived, and to fall from grace through disobedience, so an elect lady, by failing to endure to the end, can lose her chosen status."[44]

During the early days of the Church was Emma's service noteworthy?

Lucy Mack Smith wrote, "If elders were sent away to preach, [Emma] was the first to volunteer her services to assist in clothing them for their journey. Whatever her own privations, she scorned to complain."[45] When a revelation was given to Joseph commanding Parley P. Pratt, Ziba Peterson, Peter Whitmer Jr., and Oliver Cowdery to journey to Missouri, "Emma Smith and several other sisters began to make arrangements to furnish those who were set apart for this mission with the necessary clothing, which was no easy task, as the most of it had to be manufactured out of the raw material." Emma labored to provide the needed clothing even though her health was delicate at this time. "She did not favor herself on this account, but whatever her hands found to do, she did with her might, until she went so far beyond her strength that she brought upon herself a heavy fit of sickness, which lasted four weeks."[46]

Did Emma accompany Joseph from western New York to Kirtland, Ohio?

In December 1830, Joseph received a revelation commanding that he and his followers leave western New York "because of the enemy and for your sakes" (D&C 37:1). In obedience, his followers sold their houses, out-dwellings, and other possessions to migrate to Ohio. Whatever their economic circumstances, neither poverty nor discomfort could stop the flow of Mormon faithful to Ohio. So great were their numbers, one journalist announced the "whole world" would soon be living in rural Kirtland. "Every available house, shop, hut, or barn was filled to its utmost capacity. Even boxes were roughly extemporized and used for shelter until something more permanent could be secured."[47]

As for Joseph and Emma, they arrived in Kirtland about February 1, 1831. During their early days in the community, they lodged with newfound friends—Isaac Morley and Newel K. Whitney. Of this period in their lives, Lucy Mack Smith recalled that Emma "labored faithfully for the interest of those with whom she stayed, cheering them by her lively and spirited conversation."[48]

Did Emma give birth to twins in Kirtland?

While reaching out to serve others, Emma experienced her own personal suffering. Twins Louisa and Thaddeus were born on April 30, 1831, in Kirtland, but like her firstborn son, Alvin, they did not survive a day beyond their birth.

In May 1831 Joseph and Emma became the parents of twins—Joseph and Julia Murdock. Their mother had died and their father trusted their care to the Smiths. Joseph and Emma raised these newborn infants as their own—in a loving manner.

Did one of the Murdock twins die the night Joseph was tarred and feathered in Hiram, Ohio?

On the evening of March 24, 1832, Joseph and his wife Emma were caring for their eleven-month-old twins (Joseph and Julia Murdock Smith) who were ill from the effects of measles. A dozen men broke into their bedroom and grabbed at Joseph's "shirt, drawers and limbs." His struggle to free himself spawned threats of death from the lawless men. "[This] quieted me," Joseph wrote. "You will have mercy and spare my life, I hope," he pled. The profane response was, "Call on yer God for help, we'll show ye no mercy." They "beat and scratch me well, tear off my shirt and drawers, and leave me naked," Joseph said.[49] Tar and feathers followed—feathers to symbolize that these men openly mocked him and his teachings. Confident that their dark deed had left their victim dead, the lawless intruders scattered into the shadows of the night.

Although Joseph survived the abuse, his young son Joseph Smith Murdock did not. Measles, a sometimes deadly illness, was taking its toll upon the infant as was a cold that further compromised his health. Try as Joseph and Emma might, death stalked their young son. Within days of the tarring and feathering, the infant son died. Joseph Murdock Smith was the fourth child of Joseph and Emma's to pass away.

This was not the death the angry mob had planned that cold night in March. They wanted nothing less than the death of Joseph "the Mormon Prophet," not his son. Yet the mob had caused doors to gape open, exposing the seriously ill child to the frigid weather. Were they accountable? Perhaps. Regardless, it was a small gathering on March 29 that watched as the infant son was buried.

How many of Emma's children lived to adulthood?

Of the adopted Murdock twins, only Julia lived to maturity. Of the nine children Emma bore, only four grew to adulthood. In this tragedy, Joseph found hope and comfort:

> I have a father, brothers, children, and friends who have gone to a world of spirits. They are only absent for a moment. They are in the spirit, and we shall soon meet again. The time will soon ar-

Lewis Bidamon with Emma's sons—Joseph III, Alexander, Frederick, and David.

rive when the trumpet shall sound. When we depart, we shall hail our mothers, fathers, friends, and all whom we love, who have fallen asleep in Jesus. There will be no fear of mobs, persecutions, or malicious lawsuits and arrests; but it will be an eternity of felicity.[50]

He added,

> If I have no expectation of seeing my father, mother, brothers, sisters and friends again, my heart would burst in a moment, and I should go down to my grave. The expectation of seeing my friends in the morning of the resurrection cheers my soul and makes me bear up against the evils of life. It is like their taking a long journey, and on their return we meet them with increased joy.[51]

Did Emma receive heavenly comfort at the death of her children?

A few days before her own death in April 1879, Emma told her nurse, Elizabeth Revel, that Joseph came to her in a vision and said, "Emma, come with me, it is time for you to come with me." As Emma related it, she said,

> "I put on my bonnet and my shawl and went with him; I did not think that it was anything unusual. I went with him into a mansion, and he showed me through the different apartments of that beautiful mansion. And one room was the nursery. In that nursery was a babe in the cradle." She said, "I knew my babe, my Don Carlos that was taken from me." She sprang forward, caught the child up in her arms, and wept with joy over

the child. When Emma recovered herself sufficient she turned to Joseph and said, "Joseph, where are the rest of my children." He said to her, "Emma, be patient and you shall have all of your children." Then she saw standing by her side a personage of light, even the Lord Jesus Christ.[52]

Did Joseph share words of comfort with Emma during these difficult times?

A glimpse of his comfort is revealed in a personal letter written to Emma on June 6, 1832, from Greenville, Indiana. In the letter, Joseph wrote that he was confident both of them could sympathize with Hyrum [Joseph's brother] over the loss of a child:

> Dear Wife
>
> I would inform you that Brother Martin has arrived here and braught the pleasing news that our Familys were well when he left there which Greately Cheared our hearts and revived our Spirits we thank our hevenly Father for his Goodness unto us. . . I was grieved to hear that Hiram had [lost] his little Child I think we Can in Some degree Simpathise with him but we all must be reconciled to our lots and say the will [of God] be done. . . I am happy to find that you are still in the faith of Christ and at Father Smiths I hope you will Comfort Father and Mother in their trials and Hiram and Jerusha and the rest of the Family. . . I Should Like [to] See little Julia and once more take her on my knee and converse with you on all the subjects which concerns us.[53]

Did Emma's patriarchal blessing give her comfort?

In the patriarchal blessing pronounced upon Emma in 1834 by her father-in-law, Joseph Smith Sr., and scribed by Oliver Cowdery, she was comforted in three specific areas of her life. First was an acknowledgment of the suffering she had endured from the persecution Joseph had faced: "Thy soul has been afflicted because of the wickedness of men in seeking the destruction of thy companion, and thy whole soul has been drawn out in prayer for his deliverance; rejoice, for the Lord has heard thy supplications." The second was a promise of future blessing for her parental family: "Thou hast grieved for the hardness of the hearts of thy father's house, and thou hast longed for their salvation. The Lord will have respect to thy cries, and by his judgments he will cause some of them to see their folly and repent of their sins; but it will be by affliction that they will be saved." And third, was a recognition of her suffering from the loss of her babies: "Thou hast seen much sorrow because the Lord has taken from thee three of thy children: in this thou art not to be blamed, for he knows thy pure desires to raise up a family, that the name of my Son might be blessed."[54]

Although missionary travel took Joseph away from Emma for prolonged periods of time, did he show his abiding love for her through his letters?

One example of his love is an October 13, 1832, letter written from New York City. This letter not only conveys Joseph's thoughts of Emma and his concern for her, but also his love for their daughter Julia:

> This day I have been walking through the most splended part of the City of New Y – the buildings are truly great and wonderful. . . I returned to my

room to meditate and calm my mind and behold the thaughts of home of Emma and Julia rushes upon my mind like a flood and I could wish for [a] moment to be with them my breast is filld with all the feelings and tenderness of a parent and a Husband . . . I hope you will excuse me for writting this letter so soon after w[r]iting for I feel as if I wanted to say something to you to comfort you in your peculier triel and presant affliction I hope God will give you strength that you may not faint I pray God to soften the hearts of those arou[n]d you to be kind to you . . . you must cumfort yourself knowing that God is your friend in heaven and that you hav[e] one true and living friend on Earth your Husband.[55]

One of Joseph's most prolonged absences was when he marched with Zion's Camp to western Missouri. In that quasi-military setting, did he pause to write letters of love and concern to Emma?

There are two surviving letters written to Emma while on that march. On May 18, 1834, while encamped in the state of Indiana, Joseph wrote to Emma:

meeting being over I sit down in my tent to write a few lines to you to let you know that you are on my mind and that I am sensible of the dutes of a Husband and Father and that I am well and I pray God to let his blessings rest upon you and the children and all that are a round you untill I return to your society . . . I must close for I cannot write on my knees sitting on the ground to edification O may the blessings of God rest upon you is the prayre of your Husband until death.[56]

Two weeks later, on June 4, 1834, while encamped on the banks of the Mississippi River, Joseph wrote to Emma,

> I have been able to endur[e] the fatigue of the journey far beyond my most sanguine expectations, except have been troubled some with lameness, have had my feet blistered, but are now well, . . . were it not at every now and then our thoughts linger with inexpressible anxiety for our wives and our children our kindred according to the flesh who are entwined around our hearts; and also our brethren and friends; our whole journey would be as a dream, and this would be the happiest period of all our lives.[57]

Did Joseph continue to write of his unfailing love for Emma while he was a prisoner in the state of Missouri?

In a November 4, 1838 letter written while imprisoned in Independence, Missouri, Joseph penned,

> My dear and beloved companion, of my bosam, in tribulation, and affliction,
>
> I woud inform you that I am well, and that we are all of us in good spirits as regards our own fate. . . I have great anxiety about you, and my lovely children, my heart morns [and] bleeds for the brotheren, and sisters, and for the slain people of God. . . I cannot learn much for certainty in the situation that I am in, and can only pray for deliverance, untill it is meeted out. . . may God give you wisdom and prudance and sobriety which [I] have every reason to believe you will, those little [children] are subjects of my meditation continu-

ally, tell them that Father is yet alive, God grant
that he may see them again Oh Emma for God
sake do not forsake me nor the truth but remember
me, if I do [not] meet you again in this life may
God grant that we may meet in heaven, I cannot
express my feelings, my heart is full, Farwell Oh
my kind and affectionate Emma I am yours forever
your Hu[s]band and true friend.[58]

In a second letter written eight days later on November 12,
1838, while imprisoned in Richmond Jail, Joseph penned,

My Dear Emma,

we are prisoners in chains, and under strong
guards, for Christ sake and for no other cause. . .
I recieved your letter which I read over and over
again, it was a sweet morsal to me. Oh God grant
that I may have the privaliege of seeing once more
my lovely Family, in the injoyment, of the sweets of
liberty, and sotial life, to press them to my bosam
and kiss their lovely cheeks would fill my heart
with unspeakable grattitude, tell the chilldren that
I am alive and trust I shall come and see them before long, comfort their hearts all you can, and try
to be comforted yourself, all you can. . . tell little
Joseph, he must be a good boy, Father loves him
[with] a perfect love, he is the Eldest must not hurt
those that [are] smaller then him, but cumfor[t]
them tell little Frederick, Father, loves him, with
all his heart, he is a lovely boy. Julia is a lovely little
girl, I love hir also She is a promising child, tell
her Father wants her to remember him and be a
good girl. . . little Elexander is on my mind con-
tinuly Oh my affectionate Emma, I want you to

remember that I am [a] true and faithful friend, to
you and the chilldren, forever, my heart is intwined
around you[r]s forever and ever, oh my God bless
you all amen

I am your husband and am in bands and tribu-
lation &c – Joseph Smith Jr

P S write as often as you can, and if possible
come and see me, and bring the chilldren if possible.[59]

About two weeks later, while a prisoner in Liberty Jail, in a
December 1, 1838 letter, Joseph wrote:

Dear companion

I take this oppertunity to inform you that we arrived in Liberty and commited to Jaol this Evening
but we are all in good spirits Captain bogard [Sam-
uel Bogart] will hand you this line my respects to all
remain where you are at preasant yours &c –[60]

Joseph Smith was a prisoner in Liberty Jail.
Painting by C.C.A. Christensen.

On March 21, 1839, while still incarcerated in Liberty Jail, Joseph penned:

Affectionate Wife

I want to be with you very much but the powers of mobocra[c]y is to many for me at preasant. . Dear Emma I very well know your toils and simpathise with you if God will spare my life once more to have the privelege of takeing care of you I will ease your care and indeavour to cumfort your hearts I wa[n]t you to take the best care of the family you can which I believe you will do all you can I was sorry to learn that Frederick was sick but I trust he is well again and that you are all well I want you to try to gain time and write to me a long letter and tell me all you can and even if old major [the family dog] is alive yet and what those little pratlers say that cling around you[r] neck do you tell them I am in prison that their lives might be saved . . . Dear Emma do you think that my being cast into prison by the mob renders me less worthy of your friendsship no I do not think so but when I was in prisen and ye viseted me inasmuch as you have don it to the least [of] these you have don it to me these shall enter into life Eternal but no more your Husband.[61]

In yet another letter written in Liberty Jail, Joseph penned on April 4, 1839,

Dear – and affectionate – wife.

My Dear Emma I think of you and the children continualy, if I could tell you my tale, I think you would say it was altogether enough for once, to grattify the malice of hell that I have suffered. I want [to] see little Frederick, Joseph, Julia, and Alexander, Joana, and old major. And as to yourself if you want to know how much I want to see you, examine your feelings, how much you want to see me, and Judge for [yourself], I would gladly go from here to you barefoot, and bareheaded, and half naked, to see you and think it great pleasure, and never count it toil, but do not think I am babyish, for I do not feel so, I bare with fortitude all my oppression, so do those that are with me, not one of us have flinched yet, I want you [to] not let those little fellows, forgit me, tell them Father loves them with a perfect love, and he is doing all he can to git away from the mob to come to them, do teach them all you can, that they may have good minds, be tender and kind to them, dont be fractious to them, but listen to their wants, tell them Father says they must be good children, mind their mother, My Dear Emma there is great respo[n]sibility resting upon you, in preserveing yourself in honor, and sobriety, before them, and teaching them right things, to form their young and tender minds, that they begin in right paths, and not git contaminated when young, by seeing ungodly examples, I soppose you see the need of my council, and help, but combinnation [of] things have conspired to place me where I am, and I know it [is] not my fault.[62]

Did Emma and her children suffer from religious persecution due to their familial ties to Joseph?

Emma and her children were not immune from religious persecution. Joseph Smith III recalled:

I remember vividly the morning my father came to visit his family after the arrest [outside of Far West]. . . When he was brought to the house by an armed guard I ran out of the gate to greet him, but was roughly pushed away from his side by a sword in the hand of the guard and not allowed to go near him. . . My mother, also, was not permitted to approach him and had to receive his farewell by word of lip only. The guard did not permit him to pass into the house nor her to pass out, either because he heard an attempt would be made to rescue his prisoner or because of some brutal instinct in his own breast.[63]

Are any letters that Emma wrote to Joseph still in existence?

Only a few words that Emma wrote to Joseph remain. One is a letter penned on March 7, 1839, soon after she crossed the Mississippi River to get to Illinois:

I shall not attempt to write my feelings altogether, for the situation in which you are, the walls, bars, and bolts, rolling rivers, running streams, rising hills, sinking vallies and spreading prairies that separate us, and the cruel injustice that first cast you into prison and still holds you there, with many other considerations, places my feelings far beyond description. Was it not for conscious innocence, and the direct interposition of divine mercy, I am very sure I never should have been able to have endured the scenes of suffering that I have passed through, since what is called the Militia, came into Far West, under the ever to be remembered Gov-

ernor's notable order. . . We are all well at present,
except Frederick, who is quite sick. Little Alexander who is now in my arms is one of the finest little
fellows, you ever saw in your life, he is so strong
that with the assistance of a chair he will run all
round the room. . . No one but God, knows the
reflections of my mind and the feelings of my heart
when I left our house and home, and allmost all of
every thing that we possessed excepting our little
children, and took my journey out of the State of
Missouri, leaving you shut up in that lonesome
prison. But the recollection is more than human
nature ought to bear. . . The daily sufferings of our
brethren in travelling and camping out nights, and
those on the other side of the river would beggar
the most lively description. The people in this state
[Illinois] are very kind indeed, they are doing much
more than we ever anticipated they would; I have
many more things I could like to write but have not
time and you may be astonished at my bad writing and incoherent manner, but you will pardon
all when you reflect how hard it would be for you
to write, when your hands were stiffened with hard
work, and your heart convulsed with intense anxiety. But I hope there is better days to come to us
yet.[64]

Did Joseph advise Emma to confront the religious persecution and bigotry of Missouri?

Joseph taught,

> Stand fast, ye Saints of God, hold on a little
> while longer, and the storm of life will be past, and

you will be rewarded by that God whose servants
you are, and who will duly appreciate all your toils
and afflictions for Christ's sake and the Gospel's.
Your names will be handed down to posterity as
Saints of God.[65]

Joseph assured Emma and other followers:

I know that the cloud will burst, and Satan's
kingdom be laid in ruins, with all his black designs;
and that the Saints will come forth like gold seven
times tried in the fire, being made perfect through
sufferings and temptations, and that the blessings
of heaven and earth will be multiplied upon their
heads; which may God grant for Christ's sake.[66]

After fleeing Missouri, where did Emma find refuge?

Emma was among the followers of Joseph Smith who ford-
ed the icy Mississippi River seeking refuge from the effects of
the extermination order that forced Mormons to leave the state
of Missouri. With two babies, Alexander and Frederick, in her
arms and two children, Joseph and Julia, at her skirts, Emma
walked across the frozen Mississippi to reach Quincy, Illinois,
on February 15, 1839.

Attorney Orville H. Browning was among those who
witnessed the Mormon exiles, like Emma and her children,
crossing the frozen Mississippi: "Great God! have I not seen it?
Yes, my eyes have beheld the blood-stained traces of innocent
women and children, in the drear winter, who had traveled
hundreds of miles barefoot, through frost and snow, to seek a
refuge from their savage pursuers. 'Twas a scene of horror sufficient to enlist sympathy from an adamantine heart."[67]

Wilford Woodruff, seeing Emma after this ordeal, penned,
"[Emma] had passed through a scene of affliction since I last

saw her & even now Joseph her husband is in prison with other Saints through the power of Persecution."[68]

Did Emma carry a new translation of the Bible across the Mississippi River?

In addition to the babies in her arms and the two children at her skits, Emma carried Joseph's papers to Illinois. The papers contained his inspired revision of the Bible. In fact, she kept the revisions after her husband's death. On August 19, 1844, Elder Willard Richards called on "Emma Smith, widow of the Prophet, for the new translation of the *Bible*. She said she did not feel disposed to give it up at present."[69] However, Emma did allow John Bernhisel to read the new translation manuscript. He borrowed it for three months. During that interim, he copied the manuscript markings into his own Bible, which he later gave to Brigham Young. Of that experience, Bernhisel wrote,

> I had great desire to see the New Translation but did not like to ask for it; but one evening, being at Bro. Joseph's house about a year after his death, Sister Emma to my surprise asked me if I would not like to see it. I answered, yes. She handed it to me the next day, and I kept it in my custody about three months. She told me it was not prepared for the press, as Joseph had designed to go through it again. I did not copy all that was translated leaving some few additions and changes that were made in some of the books. But so far as I did copy, I did so as correctly as I could.[70]

Of her possessing the papers, Emma said, "I never had any fear that the house would burn down as long as the Inspired Translation of the Bible was in it. I always felt safe when it was in the house, for I knew it could not be destroyed."[71] Emma retained possession of the new translation until 1867 when she gave it to her son Joseph Smith III saying, "If I had trusted all that wished for that privilege [to copy them or have them] you would not have had them in your possession now."[72]

When did Joseph and Emma and their children settle in the swampland of Commerce, Illinois?

In April 1839, land speculators offered to sell Commerce, a mosquito-infested marshland, to Joseph and his followers for almost no money down. Mormon exiles could afford little more, so the purchase price of the swampland was agreed upon. In describing the purchase Joseph said, "The place was literally a wilderness. The land was mostly covered with trees and bushes, and much of it so wet that it was with the utmost difficulty a footman could get through, and totally impossible for teams." Yet with "no more eligible place presenting itself," the Latter-day Saint prophet "considered it wisdom to make an attempt to build up a city."[73] On May 10, 1839, Joseph and Emma and their small children settled in Commerce in a blockhouse known as the Homestead near the Mississippi River.

How did Joseph and Emma deal with the illnesses inherent in the swampland of Commerce?

Weakened by their ordeals in Missouri and living in make-shift tents and wagons in Commerce, thousands of Mormons fell prey to illnesses inherent in the Mississippi valley. "It was a very sickly time," wrote Wilford Woodruff. "Joseph had given up his home in Commerce to the sick, and had a tent pitched in his dooryard and was living in that himself."[74]

Lucy Mack Smith was among those who contracted the "strange fever" that infested the marshy lowlands. "I was taken very sick and was brought nigh unto death," she recalled. "For five nights Emma never left me, but stood at my bedside all the night long, at the end of which time she was overcome with fatigue and taken sick herself." Mother Smith continued, "Joseph then took her place and watched with me the five succeeding nights, as faithfully as Emma had done."[75] She added, "Joseph and Emma devoted their whole time and attention to the care of the sick during this time of distress."[76]

Why did Joseph leave Commerce and travel to Washington, D.C.?

Joseph left Commerce after most of the sickness had subsided. The purpose of his journey was to take Missouri Redress Petitions—grievances of the Latter-day Saints against the state of Missouri—to Martin Van Buren, then president of the United States.

Less than fifty miles from Commerce, Joseph wrote:

My Dear Wife

I shall be filled [with] constant anxiety about you and the children until I hear from you and in a perticular maner litle Frecerick it was so painful to leave him sick I hope you will wa[t]ch over those tender offsprings in a maner that becoming a mother and saint and try to cu[l]tivate their minds and learn [them] to read and be sober do not let [the children] be exposed to the wether to take cold and try to git all the rest you can it will be a long and lonesome time dureing my absence from you and nothing but a sense of humanity could have urged me on to so great a sacrafice but shall I see so many perish and [not] seek redress?[77]

On January 20, 1840, while he was in Philadelphia, Joseph penned:

My Dear and beloved Wife

I shall start for Washington in a few day[s] and from there home as soon as posible I am filled with constant anxiety and shall be until I git home I pray God to spare you all untill I git home my dear Emma my heart is intwined arround you and those little ones I want [you] to remember me tell all the chi[l]dren that I love them and will come home as soon as I can yours in the bonds of love your Husband u[n]till Death &c.[78]

When Joseph returned to Commerce did he once again turn his home into a resting place for the sick?

"My house has been a home and resting-place for thousands, and my family many times obliged to do without food, after having fed all they had to visitors," Joseph said. His only lament was that he could not do more for the sick or the visitor in town.

When one Latter-day Saint observed the dilemma Joseph faced with frequent guests and penniless converts and that he had reduced himself to "woman's work," he concluded the issue was home management and suggested the root of the problem was Emma. "I said to him, Brother Joseph, my wife does much more hard work than does your wife." The Prophet replied, "If a man cannot learn in this life to appreciate a wife and do his duty by her, in properly taking care of her, he need not expect to be given one in the hereafter." The flippant advisor wrote, "His words shut my mouth as tight as a clam. I took them as terrible reproof. After that I tried to do better by the good wife I had and tried to lighten her labors."[79]

On October 20, 1839, the high council "*voted* that Joseph Smith, Jun., and his family be exempt from receiving in future such crowds of visitors as have formerly thronged his house."[80]

How did Joseph feel about Emma's willingness to feed so many guests?

One night Joseph ate dinner with William W. Phelps. During the conversation, Joseph "was remarking to Brother Phelps what a kind, provident wife I had,—that when I wanted a little bread and milk, she would load the table with so many good things, it would destroy my appetite." At this point in the conversation, "Emma came in, while [William W.] Phelps, in continuation of the conversation said, 'You must do as [Napoleon] Bonaparte did—have a little table, just large enough for the victuals you want yourself.' Mrs. Smith replied, 'Mr. Smith is a bigger man than Bonaparte: he can never eat without his friends.' I remarked, 'That is the wisest thing I ever heard you say.'"[81]

Did Emma have many friends?

According to Nauvoo resident Emmeline B. Wells, "Sister Emma was benevolent and hospitable; she drew around her a large circle of friends, who were like good comrades. She was motherly in her nature to young people, always had a houseful to entertain or be entertained. She was very high-spirited and the brethren and sisters paid her great respect."[82]

Was Emma asked to compile a second hymnal for the Church in Nauvoo?

On October 27, 1839, "the High Council of Nauvoo *voted*, that Sister Emma Smith select and publish a hymn-book for the use of the Church, and that Brigham Young be informed of this action and he not publish the hymns taken by him from Commerce [to England]; and that the Council assist in publishing a hymn-book and the *Times and Seasons*."[83] In accordance with the vote, Emma compiled a second hymnal. This 1841 hymnal included 304 hymns with suggested tempos.

Did Emma own property in Nauvoo and the surrounding area?

On May 15, 1841, Emma purchased farmland in Hancock County for $2,700 from Ebenezer and Eleanor Wiggins. From that date until June 27, 1844, Emma's name, and that of her children, appeared on multiple land transactions. For example, at the time of her husband's martyrdom, she and her children owned three parcels of land outside of Nauvoo and twenty-eight parcels in town. A controversy arose over whether the properties were in actuality hers or whether they belonged to the Church. The controversy was not amicably solved. In 1847, Emma started selling her property. Her last property transaction was on July 13, 1849. The later transactions evidence plummeting property values in Nauvoo.[84]

Was Emma involved in the charitable events that preceded the organization of the Relief Society?

"Nauvoo grew, with magic rapidity, from a few rude homes to a magnificent city," penned journalist Harvey Cluff.[85] Yet, not every resident of Nauvoo prospered in the 1840s. One such man was Luman Shurtliff, a laborer in the stone quarries. "We labored ten hours a day, and got something to take to our families for supper and breakfast. Many times we got nothing," wrote Shurtliff.[86]

Sarah Melissa Kimball, wife of Hiram Kimball, witnessed the struggles of faithful stonecutters like Luman Shurtliff. She wanted to help, as did her seamstress Miss Margaret Cook. "I told [Miss Cook] I would furnish material if she would make some shirts for the workman," wrote Sarah. An agreement was made and the two women went to work to assist the poor of Nauvoo. Near neighbors saw the women's charitable acts and also expressed a desire to help. Sarah recalled, "We decided to invite a few to come and consult with us on the subject of forming a Ladies' Society" to help the poor of Nauvoo. "The neighboring sisters met in my parlor and decided to organize" on March 4, 1842.[87]

To be fully organized like other benevolent societies in the midwestern states, the group required a constitution and an election of officers. Sarah Kimball asked Eliza R. Snow to create the constitution and bylaws of the society before elections were held. Eliza wrote the proposed documents and showed the results of her efforts to Joseph Smith. He lauded her accomplishments and stated that the constitution and bylaws were "the best he had ever seen." But he told Eliza that the Lord wanted to provide "something better for [the women of Nauvoo] than a written Constitution." Said Joseph, "I will organize the women under the priesthood after the pattern of the priesthood."[88]

Was Emma the first president of the Female Relief Society of Nauvoo?

On Thursday, March 17, 1842, twenty women, from a teenager to a widow in her fifties, crowded into the upper story of a brick store on Water Street in Nauvoo. In the presence of these women, Joseph organized the Female Relief Society of Nauvoo and directed its first meeting. Thirty-eight-year-old Emma Smith was elected president of the society. Emma was then blessed and her counselors set apart by Elder John Taylor.[89]

The Female Relief Society of Nauvoo was organized in the Red Brick Store.

What was the purpose of the Female Relief Society of Nauvoo?

Perhaps Eliza R. Snow said it best: "The popular Institutions of the day should not be our guide—that as daughters of Zion, we should set an example for all the world."[90] She set forth the purpose of the society in verse:

The Female Relief Society of Nauvoo

What Is It?

It is an Institution form'd to bless
The poor, the widow, and the fatherless—
To clothe the naked and the hungry feed,
And in the holy paths of virtue, lead.

To seek out sorrow, grief and mute despair,
And light the lamp of hope eternal there—
To try the strength of consolation's art
By breathing comfort to the mourning heart.

To chase the clouds that shade the aspect, where
Distress presides; and wake up pleasures there—
With open heart extend the friendly hand
To hail the stranger, from a distant land.

To stamp a vetoing impress on each move
That Virtue's present dictates disapprove—
To put the tattler's coinage, scandal, down,
And make corruption feel its with'ring frown.

To give instruction, where instruction's voice
Will guide the feet and make the heart rejoice—
To turn the wayward from their recklessness,
And lead them in the ways of happiness.

It is an *Order*, fitted and design'd
To meet the wants of body, and of mind—
To seek the wretched, in their long abode—
Supply their wants, and raise their hearts to God.

—E. R. Snow[91]

Did Joseph Smith instruct the women of the Relief Society to be charitable to others?

Joseph admonished the women,

Consider the state of the afflicted and try to alleviate their sufferings; let your bread feed the hungry, and your clothing cover the naked; let your liberality dry up the tear of the orphan, and cheer the disconsolate widow; let your prayers, and presence, and kindness, alleviate the pains of the distressed, and your liberality contribute to their necessities; do good unto all men, especially unto the household of faith, that you may be harmless and blameless, the sons of God without rebuke. Keep the commandments of God—all that he has given, does give, or will give, and an halo of glory will shine around your path; the poor will rise up and call you blessed; you will be honored and respected by all good men; and your path will be that of the just, which shineth brighter and brighter until the perfect day.[92]

Joseph added,

Though I speak with the tongues of men and angels, and have not charity, I am become as sounding brass, or a tinkling cymbal; and said, don't be limited in your views with regard to your

neighbor's virtue, but beware of self-righteous-
ness, and be limited in the estimate of your own
virtues, and not think yourselves more righteous
than others; you must enlarge your souls towards
each other, if you would do like Jesus, and carry
your fellow-creatures to Abraham's bosom. He said
he had manifested long-suffering, forbearance and
patience towards the Church, and also to his enemies; and we must bear with each other's failings,
as an indulgent parent bears with the foibles of his
children.[93]

Joseph challenged the women to search out the needy and
minister to their needs: "This is according to your natures,"
he told the sisters "it is natural for females to have feelings of
charity—you are now plac'd in a situation where you can act
according to those sympathies which God has planted in your
bosoms. If you live up to these principles how great and glo-
rious! If you live up to your privileges, the angels cannot be
restrained from being your associates."[94]

He then said, "This is the beginning of better days for the
poor and needy, who shall be made to rejoice and pour forth
blessings on your heads."[95]

Did Emma fulfill Joseph's vision for the Relief Society?

Emma, perceiving a need for greater service by the women
of her society, stated, "We are going to do something *extraordinary*—when a boat is stuck on the rapids, with a multitude
of Mormons on board, we shall consider that a loud call for
relief—we expect extraordinary occasions and pressing calls."[96]
Instead of waiting for calls of distress, Emma encouraged the
women to search for those in need. She noted that Philindia
Myrick, a widow caring for three children, was "industrious—

performs her work well, [and] therefore recommend[ed] her to the patronage of such as wish to hire needlework."[97] Emma "hired a poor man to plough and fence father Knights lot at $22.60, and solicited the Society in behalf of the payment which might be made in provision, clothing, and furniture."[98]

Emma's example of helping the poor and blessing their lives was emulated by society members. Sister Pratt suggested that the society help Brother Henderson, a needy widower with nine children who was "an industrious, and worthy person." Sister Durfee asked the society to "unite like the ancient saints in faith & pray'r" for Porter Rockwell's deliverance from a Missouri jail. Patty Sessions spoke of a man whose appearance "bespoke deep poverty" and offered to donate pantaloons and a shirt and hoped others could do more.[99]

Within each Relief Society unit, Emma organized "necessity committees" or visiting neighbors to look after the needs of the poor and call upon those with means to relieve the suffering of the disadvantaged. Under Emma's guidance, women of the society blessed many through their unselfish service. Heavy burdens were lifted, sorrows too severe to be carried alone were shared, and necessities needed to sustain life were freely proffered. Employment was secured, temporary housing obtained, and clothing and provisions were provided to sustain life in Nauvoo.

Did the Relief Society help Joseph and Emma during their times of need?

The society petitioned Governor Thomas Carlin of Illinois for assistance in halting lawsuits and malignant gossip that so often confronted Joseph Smith. In July 1842, Emma Smith, Amanda Barns Smith, and Eliza R. Snow went to Quincy to meet with the governor. Eliza wrote in her diary on July 29:

> Just returned from Quincy, where I visited the

governor in company with Mrs. Emma Smith who presented him a petition from the Female Relief Society. The governor received us with cordiality, and as much affability and politeness as his excellency is a master of, assuring us of his protection, by saying that the laws and constitution of our country shall be his polar star in case of any difficulty. He manifested much friendship, and it remains for time and circumstance to prove the sincerity of his profession.[100]

Joseph expressed gratitude to these sisters of the society for taking a "most active part in my welfare against my enemies." He then said, "God loves you, and your prayers in my behalf shall avail much: let them not cease to ascend to God continually, in my behalf."[101]

From October 1842 through winter 1843, when Emma had succumbed to chills and fever, women of the society attended to her needs. Eliza R. Snow wrote of the care Emma received from Mrs. Durfee:

> Sir, for your consolation permit me to tell
> That your Emma is *better*—she soon will be well;
> Mrs. Durfee stands by her, night & day like a friend
> And is prompt every call—every wish to attend;
> Then pray for your Emma, but indulge not a fear
> For the God of our forefathers, smiles on us here.[102]

In what way did the Relief Society prepare women to receive an endowment—a gift from God?

Joseph taught the women of the Relief Society about the sacred doctrines of temple worship. At one society meeting, he said, "I now turn the key in your behalf in the name of the Lord, and this Society shall rejoice, and knowledge and intelligence shall flow down from this time, henceforth." Turning the key led to more prophetic discussions of gospel principles, the sharing of testimonies, and a greater desire to receive an endowment from God. Lucy Mack Smith, a frequent participant in these discussions, remarked, "This institution is a good one . . . we must cherish one another, watch over one another, comfort one another, and gain instruction, . . . that we may all sit down in heaven together."[103]

Did Joseph and Emma receive the blessings of the endowment?

Joseph and Emma enjoyed the blessings of the endowment and of being sealed for all eternity. They also liked to spend time together. Emmeline B. Wells recalled, "Emma Smith was fond of horses and could manage them well in riding or driving. Many can recall seeing her mounted on horseback beside her husband in military parades and a grander couple could nowhere be found."[104] Joseph was at Emma's bedside on more than one occasion. "Emma began to be sick with fever; consequently I kept in the house with her all day," he wrote in his journal.[105] On October 3, 1842, he penned, "Emma was a little better. I was with her all day." On October 4, he explained, "Emma is very sick again. I attended with her all the day, being somewhat poorly myself." The next day he recorded, "My dear Emma was worse, Many fears were entertained that she would not recover. . . I was unwell, and much troubled on account of Emma's sickness."[106] Mercy Thompson wrote of Joseph's care of Emma: "I saw him by the bed-side of Emma, his wife, in sickness, exhibiting all the solicitude and sympathy possible for the tenderest of hearts and the most affectionate of natures to feel."[107]

Did Joseph continue to write of his love for Emma and their children during the Nauvoo era?

In each of the letters that Joseph wrote to Emma, he expressed his concern and love for her and their little ones. His personal writings of August 1842, while hiding from Missouri pursuers, epitomizes his joy in her companionship:

> What unspeakable delight, and what transports of joy swelled my bosom, when I took by the hand, on that night [August 11, 1842] my beloved Emma—she that was my wife, even the wife of my youth, and the choice of my heart. Many were the reverberations of my mind when I contemplated for a moment the many scenes we had been called to pass through, the fatigues and the toils, the sorrows and sufferings, and the joys and consolations, from time to time, which had strewed our paths and crowned our board. Oh what a commingling of thought filled my mind for the moment, again she is here, even in the seventh trouble—undaunted, firm, and unwavering—unchangeable, affectionate Emma![108]

Days later he again wrote of his love for Emma and the children:

> My Dear Emma
>
> I embrace this opportunity to express to you some of my feelings this morning. First of all, I take the liberty to tender you my sincere thanks for the two interesting and consoling visits that you have made me during my almost exiled situation. Tongue cannot express the gratitude of my heart, for the warm and true-hearted friendship you have manifested in these things toward me. The time has passed away

since you left me, very agreeably; thus far, my mind being perfectly reconciled to my fate, let it be what it may. . . I think if I could have a respite of about six months with my family, it would be a savor of life unto life; with my house. Nevertheless if it were possible I would like to live here in peace and wind up my business; . . . Tell the children that it is well with their father, as yet; and that he remains in fervent prayer to Almighty God for the safety of himself, and for you, and for them. . . Yours in haste, your affectionate husband until death, through all eternity forevermore, Joseph Smith

Is there any evidence that Joseph relied upon Emma to protect him from untoward persecution?

On August 17, 1842, Emma wrote to Illinois Governor Thomas Carlin, "Pleading the Cause of the Prophet and the People of Nauvoo." A portion of her letter reads:

May I entreat your Excellency to lighten the hand of oppression and persecution which is laid upon me and my family, which materially affect the peace and welfare of this whole community. . . And now I appeal to your Excellency, as I would unto a father, who is not only able but willing to shield me and mine from every unjust persecution. I appeal to your sympathies, and beg you to spare me and my helpless children. I beg you to spare my innocent children the heart-rending sorrow of again seeing their father unjustly dragged to prison, or to death.

Respectfully, your most obedient,

Emma Smith.[109]

It was reported that "the governor read the letter [from Emma] with much attention, apparently; and when he got through, he passed high encomiums on Emma Smith, and expressed astonishment at the judgment and talent manifest in the manner of her address."[110]

After receiving his timely response, Emma again wrote to Governor Carlin: "And now I entreat your honor to bear with me patiently while I ask what good can accrue to this state or the United States, . . . to continue this persecution upon this people, or upon Mr. Smith—a persecution that you are well aware, is entirely without any just foundation or excuse?"[111]

When did Emma first participate in baptisms for the dead?

By 1843, some of the persecution Joseph had known subsided, but only for a brief time. It was during that interim that Joseph returned to the Mansion House and resided with his family. In 1843, near the time of his return, Emma was baptized by proxy for her father Isaac Hale, mother Elizabeth Lewis Hale, sister Phebe Roote, aunt Esther Hale, uncle Reuben Hale, and great-aunt Eunice Cady.[112]

Did Joseph evidence concern for Emma's security as well as his own as persecution escalated in June 1844?

On June 23, 1844, while hiding in Iowa, Joseph wrote a quick note about his temporal affairs and his concern for Emma and their children:

> Brother Lewis has some money of mine – H.C. Kimball has $1000, in his hand of mine, Br J[ohn] Neff, Lancaster Co, Pa., - $400, You may sell the Quincy Property. – or any property that belongs to me you can find any thing about, for your support and children & mother. Do not dispair – If god

ever opens a door that is possible for me I will see you again. . . May God Almighty bless you & the children & Mother & all my friends.[113]

Was it Emma's response to this previous letter (June 23, 1844) that led Joseph to leave Iowa, return to Nauvoo, and go to Carthage?

The official *History of the Church* reports on June 23, 1844, at 1 p.m., "Emma sent over Orrin P. Rockwell, requesting him to entreat of Joseph to come back [from Iowa]. Reynolds Cahoon accompanied [Rockwell] with a letter which Emma had written to the same effect, insisting that Cahoon should persuade Joseph to come back and give himself up."[114] Benjamin F. Johnson, in a brief journal entry, confirms the report: "Through the persuasion and reproaches of his wife, Emma, and others [Joseph] was induced to return and give himself up to the slaughter."[115]

It appears that Emma and some of her friends believed the citizens of Nauvoo would be harmed if Joseph remained in Iowa. They encouraged him to return, submit to the law, and face an arraignment in Carthage on the trumped up charge of riot. With resignation Joseph said,

> If my life is of no value to my friends it is of none to myself. . . *I am going like a lamb to the slaughter, but I am calm as a summer's morning. I have a conscience void of offense toward God and toward all men. If they take my life I shall die an innocent man, and my blood shall cry from the ground for vengeance, and it shall be said of me "He was murdered in cold blood!"*[116]

Did Joseph write to Emma after he went to Carthage and was arrested on the charge of treason?

On June 25, 1844, about 2:30 p.m., Joseph wrote to Emma: "I have had an interview with Gov. Ford & he treats us honorably Myself & Hyrum have been again arrested for Treason because we called out the Nauvoo Legion but when the truth comes out we have nothing to fear."[117]

Two days later, on June 27 at about eight o'clock in the morning, Joseph penned:

Dear Emma

There is one principle which is Eternal, it is the duty of all men to protect their lives and the lives of their households whenever [it] requires. and no power has a right to forbid it. should the last extreme arrive, - but I anticipate no such extreme, - but caution is the parent of safety. –

I am very much resigned to my lot knowing I am justified and have done the best that could be done give my love to the children and all my Friends Mr Brower and all who inquire after me and as for treason I know that I have not commited any and they cannot prove one apearance of any thing of the kind So you need not have any fears that any harme can happen to us on that score may God bless you all Amen.[118]

How did Emma learn of Joseph's death?

On the evening of the martyrdom (June 27, 1844), Emma learned of the brutal murder of her husband and his brother Hyrum from her nephew Lorenzo Wasson. Official word was sent soon after daybreak the next day:

CARTHAGE Jail, 8:05 o'clock, p.m., June 27th, 1844

Joseph and Hyrum are dead. Taylor wounded, not very badly. I am well. Our guard was forced, as we believe, by a band of Missourians from 100 to 200. The job was done in an instant, and the party fled toward Nauvoo instantly. This is as I believe it. The citizens here [Carthage] are afraid of the Mormons attacking them. I promise them no!

W[illard] Richards. John Taylor.[119]

What was Emma's reaction upon seeing the remains of her husband?

About 8 a.m. on Friday, June 28, the remains of Joseph and Hyrum were placed in rough boxes, put into two wagons, and then covered with prairie hay, blankets, and bushes to protect them from the hot sun. A guard of eight soldiers led by Samuel H. Smith was detached to escort the remains to Nauvoo. Between 2:30 and 3 p.m. the funeral procession moved along Mulholland Street, where the assembled Nauvoo Legion, the city council, and thousands of mourners vented their sorrow.

The procession moved slowly into the city, passing by the unfinished temple, where additional crowds had gathered. The procession then turned down Main Street to go to the Mansion House, where the bodies were taken into the dining room and the door closed. Inside the house the bodies were washed by Dimick B. Huntington, William Marks, and William D. Huntington in preparation for the public viewing. Camphor-soaked cotton was placed in each gunshot wound, and the bodies were dressed in "fine plain drawers and shirt, white neckerchiefs, white cotton stockings and white shrouds."[120]

Widows of the deceased, Emma Smith and Mary Fielding

Smith, were among the first to view the bodies. As Emma saw the remains of Joseph, it was reported that she hesitated for a moment before saying, "Now I can see him; I am strong now." She then walked to where he lay "kneeled down, clasped him around his face and sank upon his body. She exclaimed, Joseph, Joseph, are you dead? Have the assassins shot you." According to Joseph Smith III, Emma cried, "Oh, Joseph Joseph! My husband, my husband! Have they taken you from me at last!"[121]

Eliza R. Snow poetically wrote of the grief that day in the Mansion House and on the streets of Nauvoo. Two stanzas from one of her poems read:

> All hearts with sorrow bleed, and ev'ry eye
> Is bath'd in tears—each bosom heaves a sigh—
> Hart broken widows' agonizing groans
> Are mingled with the helpless orphans' moans!
>
> Ye Saints! be still, and know that God is just—
> With steadfast purpose in his promise trust.
> Girded with sackcloth, own his mighty hand,
> And wait his judgments on this guilty land![122]

Where were the martyrs' bodies buried?

The remains of Joseph Smith and his brother Hyrum were buried in the basement of the north wing of the Nauvoo House. In fall 1844, Emma requested that their remains be removed by Dimick B. Huntington, William D. Huntington, Jonathan H. Homes, and Gilbert Goldsmith. The reburial of the bodies was 38 feet south and 20 feet west of the southwest corner of the Homestead under the floor of a small shed called a "bee house" or "spring house." Joseph III recalled seeing the second burial and watching as a lock of hair was cut from his father's head. The lock was given to Emma. She placed the hair in a locket that she wore the remainder of her life.[123]

Was a child born to Emma after the death of Joseph?

Emma gave birth to David Hyrum Smith on November 17, 1844, in Nauvoo. Eliza R. Snow, after seeing the newborn son, composed a poem commemorating his birth. A few stanzas read:

Sinless as celestial spirits—
Lovely as a morning flow'r,
Comes the smiling infant stranger
in an evil-omen'd hour.

Emma Smith and infant son, David Hyrum Smith.

In an hour of lamentation—
In a time—a season when
Zion's noblest sons are fallen,
By the hands of wicked men.

Not to share a father's fondness—
Not to know a father's worth—
By the arm of persecution
'Tis an orphan at its birth!

Smile, sweet babe! thou art unconscious
Of thy great, untimely loss!
The broad stroke of thy bereavement,
Zion's pathway seem'd to cross!

Thou may'st draw from love and kindness
All a mother can bestow;
But alas! on earth, a father
Thou art destin'd not to know![124]

Did Emma make any preparations to follow Brigham Young to the western wilderness?

In 1845, thousands of Mormons in and around Nauvoo presented a most unusual dichotomy—an oddity of grand proportions. With dogged determination, they worked to complete the temple, their homes, and their shops and to cultivate their farms. Yet those who built the city also scurried to build wagons to transport themselves and their families to regions unknown and uncharted in the Rocky Mountains. There is no historical evidence that Emma became involved in either the building of the community in 1845 or the preparations to leave Nauvoo for the West.

Did any of the thousands of Latter-day Saints who left Nauvoo for the uncharted wilderness stop to bid Emma farewell?

As the Latter-day Saints made preparations to leave Nauvoo in 1846, several took the time to go to Carthage, the county seat, and make an official record of their gift of property to Emma for "$1 and love and consideration." Such generosity resulted in her becoming a principal landowner in Nauvoo at the time of the Mormon exodus.

In addition, many Latter-day Saints visited with Emma before joining the Mormon exodus. Some wrote letters expressing their love to her. For example, John Bernhisel penned,

> Dear Sister Emma,
>
> I cannot take my departure from this place, without acknowledging the debt of gratitude that I am under to you. And in making this acknowledgement, I especially desire to be understood that I am observing no more form or idle custom, nor empty ceremony. During the three years that I was

a member of your family, I found every necessary provided for my comfort, with much order and neatness, and from yourself and family I experienced not only kindness and respect, but such affectionate regard, tenderness and delicacy as to make me feel more than your grateful friend—I may never be permitted to pay you all; but the bond of obligation shall ever remain binding on my heart and life. And I beg you to accept my profound and grateful acknowledgments for your uniform kindness and attention to me, and for your trouble of me during so long a period; and I fervently pray that God may reward you in this world a thousand-fold and in the world to come with life everlasting.[125]

Why did Emma choose not follow Brigham Young to the West?

Parley P. Pratt Jr. and Nels Madsen spoke with Emma after the Mormon exodus.

> Pratt: Do you believe that your husband Joseph Smith died true to his profession?

> Emma: I believe he was everything he professed to be.

As their discussion continued, Emma said, "You may think I was not a very good Saint not to go West, but I had a home here and I did not go because I did not know what I should have there."[126] It is important to note that she had young children to care for, so having a home was important.

After the Latter-day Saints left Nauvoo, did Emma renounce her testimony of the prophetic calling of Joseph Smith and the coming forth of the Book of Mormon?

On December 9, 1845, the *New York Sun* printed a November 20, 1845, letter signed by Emma Smith. The letter renounced Joseph Smith as a prophet and also the angelic coming forth of the Book of Mormon. Although General James Arlington Bennett of New York pronounced the letter authentic, Emma declared the letter to be a forgery. Her response to the forged letter was sent to the editor of the *New York Sun*.

> Sir:
>
> I wish to inform you, and the public through your paper, that the letter published Tuesday morning, December 9th, is a forgery, the whole of it, and I hope that this notice will put a stop to all such communications.
>
> Emma Smith.

Her denial was never printed in the *Sun*. It did, however, appear in the *Times and Seasons* on January 15, 1846.[127]

Did Emma leave town during the September 1846 Battle of Nauvoo?

Mansion House, home of Emma Smith from 1843 to 1871.

It is not a coincidence that Emma left Nauvoo with her five children on September 12, 1846, two days after the Battle of Nauvoo had begun. During that battle, she saw fire char the Mansion House.

Seeking refuge, Emma and her children boarded the steamer *Uncle*

Toby bound for Fulton, Illinois. After a six-day journey aboard the steamer, she and her family disembarked at Fulton, forty miles north of Rock Island. In Fulton, a town of fewer than five hundred residents, she rented a house near the edge of town rather than return to Nauvoo after the battle. Of their time in Fulton, Joseph Smith III recalled, "During the sojourn of our family at Fulton City, from September 1846 until February 1847, my sister Julia and I were well received in the younger social circles of that little town. A love for social functions was awakened at that time within me and from the date of our return to Nauvoo, I mingled freely in the society of the place."[128]

With Emma away and most of the Latter-day Saints having left town, did Nauvoo become a ghost town?

Thomas L. Kane visited Nauvoo soon after the Battle of Nauvoo. Of his visit, he recorded,

> I procured a skiff, and rowing across the river, landed at the chief wharf of the city. No one met me there. I looked, and saw no one. I could hear no one move; though the quiet everywhere was such that I heard the flies buzz, and the water-ripples break against the shallow of the beach. I walked through the solitary streets. The town lay as in a dream, under some deadening spell of loneliness, from which I almost feared to wake it. For plainly it had not slept long. There was no grass growing up in the paved ways. Rains had not entirely washed away the prints of dusty footsteps.
>
> Yet I went about unchecked. I went into empty workshops, ropewalks, and smithies. The spinner's wheel was idle; the carpenter had gone from his work-bench and shavings, his unfinished sash and

casing. Fresh bark was in the tanner's vat, and the fresh-chopped lightwood stood piled against the baker's oven. The blacksmith's shop was cold; but his coal heap and lading pool and crooked water horn were all there, as if he had just gone off for a holiday. No work people anywhere looked to know my errand.[129]

This emptiness is all the more noteworthy because Nauvoo had been a large city in the state, with a population of 11,500 in 1845.

Did Nauvoo regain its prominence as the years passed?

English journalist Charles Lanman recalled coming to Nauvoo a few years after the visit of Thomas L. Kane:

When this city was in its glory, every dwelling was surrounded with a garden . . . but now all the fences are in ruin, and lately crowded streets actually rank with vegetation. Of the houses left standing, not more than one out of ten was occupied, excepting by the spider and the toad. Hardly a window retained a full pane of glass, and the doors were broken, and open, and hingeless. Not a single laughing voice did I hear in the whole place, and the lines of suffering and care, seemed to be imprinted on the faces of the very children who met me in the way.[130]

Joseph Smith III wrote of the conditions of Nauvoo after the Mormon exodus:

From 1846 to as late as 1855, Nauvoo which once enjoyed a good reputation, was a place of disgrace and disorder. Saloons were many and ran wide open, proprietors and patrons alike being shiftless, thieving, drinking boisterous and thoroughly unprofitable citizens. Among the boarders at our hotel could be found men of all classes. Considerable transient traffic moved to and fro up and down the river, and the Mansion drew its share of this sort of public patronage. In the winter season we usually had, in addition to regular boarders, numbers of such patrons whom we termed "river men."[131]

The once proud city was draped in blight and crumbling ruin. Few remained to mourn her loss.

Why did Emma and her children return to Nauvoo when prospects for the town's future were so dim?

When Emma learned that Abram Van Tuyl, the man who had rented the Mansion House, was planning to vacate the house and take her furniture, she and her children returned in haste to Nauvoo. She said, "I have no friend but God, and no place to go but home."[132]

Emma resided in the Mansion House until 1871. In that year, she moved into a newly constructed two-story brick building on the southwest corner of the original foundation of the Nauvoo House. For her remaining years, Emma ran the brick building as a hotel.

Did Emma marry again?

Emma was married to Lewis Bidamon on December 23, 1847, by William Haney, a Methodist minister. Sarah M. Kimball, in a letter to Marinda Nancy Hyde, wrote of the wedding. "The marriage of Mrs. Smith is the all absorbing topic of conversation," penned Sarah:

She was married last thursday eve the groom
Mr. Bidimen [He] is I believe looked upon with
universal contempt he was a widower wears a wig
[and] married Emmy [Emma] for her property. . .
The bride was dressed in plum colored sattin a lace
tuck hankerchief gold watch & chain no cap hair
plain. . . The eve brought a grand shiveree & the
follow[ing] night a ball was given.[133]

Who was Lewis Bidamon?

"Major" Lewis Crum Bidamon was born on January 16,
1804, in Smithfield, Virginia [Williamsport, West Virginia].
For a time, he resided in Highland County, Ohio. In 1827, at
age twenty-five, he married Nancy Sebree. In 1842, he married
widow Mary Ann Douglas. This marriage failed. He was a lieu-
tenant colonel in the 32nd Regiment of Illinois Infantry. In spring
1847, Lewis moved to Nauvoo. At the time, he was forty-five
years old, a Deist by persuasion, and the father of two daughters—Zerelda and Mary Elizabeth. In December 1847, he married Emma Smith. Due to financial difficulties, in 1849 Lewis
left Nauvoo bound for the gold fields of California. Emma, a
bride of eighteen months, described the length of his absence as
"gloomy solitude." Lewis returned to Nauvoo in summer 1850.
In 1864, Lewis's marital infidelity resulted in the birth of an
illegitimate child: Charles Edward Bidamon, born March 16,
1864. In 1868, Emma allowed the child and his mother, Nancy
Perriman Brooks Abercrombie, to reside in the Mansion House.
Following Emma's death , Lewis married Nancy Abercrombie
on May 28, 1880. Lewis is remembered as leading the Fourth
of July parades in Nauvoo. The last three years of his life, he was
unable to lead the parades due to senility. He died on February
11, 1891. After his death, his widow Nancy moved to Kansas
City, Missouri, where she died on July 30, 1903.[134]

Did Emma write to Lewis during his absence in California?

Emma corresponded with Lewis when he traveled to the gold fields. A January 7, 1850, letter reads in part:

> My dear Lewis,
>
> I have scarcely enjoyed any good thing since you left home, in consequence of the terrifying apprehension that you might be suffering for the most common comfort of life. I have never been weary without thinking that you might be much more so. I never have felt the want of food without fear that you might be almost or quite starving and I have never [been] thirsty without feeling my heart sicken with the reflection that perhaps you were sinking, faint and famished for want of that reviving draught that I could obtain so easily and use so freely, and I have much feared that the heat of the sun on those burning plains might seriously affect you. But now these anxieties are over, [Emma had received a letter from Lewis] and some may think that I might be content, but I am not, neither can I be untill you are within my grasp, then, and not till then shall I be free from fears for your safety, and anxieties for your wellfare.[135]

What was the relationship between Emma and Lewis Bidamon's illegitimate son?

On September 9, 1940, Charles Edward Bidamon penned a tribute to Emma.

> I was taken into the home of Emma Smith Bidamon in 1868, at the age of four years, and was

considered as one of the family up to and including the year of her death in 1879.

> As to my recollection of her, she was a person of very even temper. I never heard her say an unkind word, or raise her voice in anger or contention. She was loved and respected by the entire community, (all who knew her). And at her funeral, which the whole countryside attended, many tears flowed, showing grief at her passing. She had a queenly bearing without the arrogance of a queen. A noble woman, showing and living a charity for all. Loving and beloved. . .
>
> Her children and grandchildren visited her ofttimes and loved and esteemed her highly. But I was there continually from the age of four in 1868 until her death in 1879, a period of eleven years. I should know her disposition and character thoroughly. Her ideals were high and her disposition kindly.[136]

Did Emma teach her children about religion and Mormonism?

On one occasion, Emma said, "I have always avoided talking to my children about having anything to do in the church, for I have suffered so much I have dreaded to have them take any part in it."[137] Yet David Hyrum Smith poetically wrote of his mother teaching her children to pray:

> Remember how she taught us five
> In faithfulness to pray
> That God would guard us through the night
> And watch us through the day.[138]

Did Emma care for her former mother-in-law Lucy Mack Smith in her declining years?

In 1851, Lucy Mack Smith moved into the Mansion House with Emma and her children. Lucy resided in the eastern part of the house for about five years. When she could no longer walk due to crippling arthritis, Lewis Bidamon made a wheelchair for her. Lucy died on May 14, 1856, at age eighty-one. The care Emma gave her mother-in-law exemplified Joseph's teaching of the need to care for aged loved ones:

> When we reflect with what care, and with what unremitting diligence our parents have striven to watch over us, and how many hours of sorrow and anxiety they have spent, over our cradles and bedsides, in times of sickness, how careful we ought to be of their feelings in their old age! It cannot be a source of sweet reflection to us, to say or do anything that will bring their gray hairs down with sorrow to the grave.[139]

Did Emma join the Reorganized Church of Jesus Christ of Latter Day Saints?

On April 6, 1860, Emma accompanied her twenty-seven-year-old son Joseph Smith III to a ten o'clock meeting held at the Mechanics' Hall in Amboy, Illinois. At the meeting, her son was acknowledged as the leader of the Reorganized Church of Jesus Christ of Latter Day Saints (RLDS, today known as the Church of Christ). At the same meeting, fifty-six-year-old Emma Smith Bidamon was received as a member of the Reorganization.

Emma was a participating member of the RLDS Church the remainder of her life. She selected hymns for the first RLDS hymnal published in 1861 as *The Latter Day Saints' Selection of*

Hymns. The hymnal included 249 texts. Members of the RLDS Olive Branch met in the Red Brick Store on Emma's property in Nauvoo.

Did each of Emma's children affiliate with the RLDS Church?

Julia Murdock Smith (May 1, 1831–September 12, 1880) did not affiliate with the RLDS Church. On November 9, 1857, she was baptized into the Catholic faith in the Church of St. Francis Xavior at St. Louis.[140]

Joseph Smith III (November 6, 1832–December 10, 1914) served as the leader of the RLDS Church for fifty-four years.[141]

Frederick Granger Williams Smith (June 20, 1836–April 13, 1862) did not affiliate with the RLDS Church.

Alexander Hale Smith (June 2, 1838–August 12, 1909) served as an apostle, presiding patriarch, and counselor to his brother Joseph III in the presidency of the RLDS Church.

David Hyrum Smith (November 17, 1844–August 29, 1904) served as an apostle and a member of the Presidency of the RLDS Church. On January 22, 1877, David was admitted to the Illinois State Asylum, where he resided the remainder of his life. It was not until April 11, 1885, however, that Joseph Smith III released him from his ecclesiastical positions in the RLDS Church.[142]

Was Emma blamed for the actions of her children in promoting the RLDS Church?

On October 7, 1869, in the Tabernacle in Salt Lake City, Orson Pratt said, "That same woman [Emma Smith Bidamon] . . . has instilled the bitterest principles of apostasy into their minds [her sons], to fight against the Church that has come to these mountains according to the predictions of Joseph."[143]

On August 24, 1872, in Farmington, Utah, Brigham Young is reported to have said:

> We would be very glad to have the privilege of saying that the children of Joseph Smith, Junior, the Prophet of God, were firm in the faith of the Gospel, and following in the footsteps of their father. But what are they doing? Trying to blot out every vestige of the work their father performed on the earth. Their mission is to endeavor to obliterate every particle of his doctrine, his faith and doings. These boys are not following Joseph Smith, but Emma Bideman. Every person who hearkens to what they say, hearkens to the will and wishes of Emma Bideman. The boys, themselves, have no will, no mind, no judgment independent of their mother. I do not want to talk about them. I am sorry for them, and I have my own faith in regard to them. I think the Lord will find them by and by.[144]

Following Joseph's death, Brigham and Emma disagreed over many things relating to Church affairs.

Did Emma retain any positive relationships with Latter-day Saints who followed Brigham Young to the West?

Many Latter-day Saints, on their way to or from mission assignments, stopped in Nauvoo and rented a room in the Mansion House from her. As the hostess of these missionaries, Emma surely had several conversations with them. However, only a few of these have been reported. For example, in 1853, artist Frederick Piercy reported, "I will say, that during some conversation which I had with persons in the neighborhood,

I found that the whole family had obtained a most excellent reputation for integrity and industry."[145]

The most remembered LDS visitors were her nephews Joseph F. Smith and Samuel H. B. Smith. When Emma's son Frederick asked, "Mother, do you know these young men?" Joseph F. Smith recalled, "She appeared to have forgotten Samuel but me She said she would have known anywhere because I looked so much like Father!!"[146]

Did Emma disagree with her LDS guests' belief in the doctrine of plural marriage?

In April 1867, Jason T. Briggs, a member of the RLDS Church, reported an interview he had with Emma Smith Bidamon. His report was printed in *The History of the Reorganized Church of Jesus Christ of Latter Day Saints*. In the interview, Briggs asked Emma about polygamy. Her answer, according to Briggs, greatly differed from her LDS guests.

"J. W. Briggs—Mrs. Bidamon, have you seen the revelation on polygamy, published by Orson Pratt, in the *Seer*, in 1852?

"Mrs. B.—I have.

"J. W. B.—Have you read it?

"Mrs. B.—I have read it, and heard it read.

"J. W. B.—Did you ever see that document in manuscript, previous to its publication, by Pratt?

"Mrs. B.—I never did.

"J. W. B.—Did you ever see any document of that kind, purporting to be a revelation, to authorize polygamy?

"Mrs. B.—No; I never did.

"J. W. B.—Did Joseph Smith ever teach you the principles of polygamy, as being revealed to him, or as a correct and righteous principle?

"Mrs. B.—He never did.

"J. W. B.—What about that statement of Brigham Young, that you burnt the original manuscript of that revelation?

"Mrs. B.—It is false in all its parts, *made out of the whole cloth*, without any foundation in truth."[147]

Did Brigham Young believe that Emma burned the document on which the revelation on plural marriage was written?

On October 11, 1874, at the semi-annual conference of the LDS Church held at the new Tabernacle in Salt Lake City, Brigham Young said:

> Emma took that revelation, supposing she had all there was; but Joseph had wisdom enough to take care of it, and he had handed the revelation to Bishop Whitney, and he wrote it all off. After Joseph had been to Bishop Whitney's he went home, and Emma began teasing for the revelation. Said she—"Joseph, you promised me that revelation, and if you are a man of your word you will give it to me." Joseph took it from his pocket and said—"Take it." She went to the fire-place and put it in, and put the candle under it and burnt it, and she thought that was the end of it.[148]

Did Emma believe that it was Brigham Young who introduced plural marriage into the Church?

On May 14, 1882, at a Sunday meeting held in the Tabernacle in Salt Lake City, Wilford Woodruff said:

Emma Smith, the widow of the Prophet, is said to have maintained to her dying moments that her husband had nothing to do with the patriarchal order of marriage, but that it was Brigham Young that got that up. I bear record before God, angels and men that Joseph Smith received that revelation; and I bear record that Emma Smith gave her husband in marriage [to] several women while he was living, some of whom are to-day living in this city, and some may be present in this congregation, and who, if called upon, would confirm my words.[149]

Did the controversy between LDS and RLDS leaders lead Emma to deny her testimony of Joseph Smith's prophetic calling?

Although she took issue with the doctrine of plural marriage, Emma never denied her testimony of Joseph's prophetic calling. In her seventy-fourth year, she said, "I believe he was everything he professed to be."[150]

Did Emma respond to questions about her relationship with Joseph Smith and her testimony of his prophetic calling near the end of her life?

Joseph Smith III interviewed his mother on February 4 through 10, 1879, just two months before her death. At the time, Joseph III was the senior editor of the *Saints' Herald*, a newspaper printed by the RLDS Church. The interview was subsequently printed in that newspaper as follows:

In a conversation held in the Herald Office during the early days of the present year, between Bishop Rogers, Elders W. W. Blair, H. A. Stebbins and a few others, leading minds in the Church, it was thought advisable to secure from Mother Bidamon, (Sister Emma Smith), her testimony upon certain points upon which various opinions existed; and to do this, it was decided to present to her a few prominent questions, which were penned and agreed upon, the answers to which might, so far as she was concerned, settle these differences of opinion. In accordance with this understanding the Senior Editor of the HERALD visited Nauvoo, in February last, arriving on the 4th and remaining until the 10th. Sister Emma answered the questions freely and in the presence of her husband, Major Lewis C. Bidamon, who was generally present in their sitting-room where the conversation took place. We were more particular in this, because it had been frequently stated to us: "Ask your mother, she knows." "Why don't you ask your mother; she dare not deny these things." "You do not dare to ask your mother!"

Our thought was, that if we had lacked courage to ask her, because we feared the answers she might give, we would put aside that fear; and, whatever the worst might be, we would hear it. The result is given below; it having been decided to give the statements to the readers of the HERALD, in view of the death of Sister Emma having occurred so soon after she made them, thus giving them the character of a last testimony.

It is intended to incorporate these questions and answers in the forthcoming history of the Reorganization.

We apologize to our mother for putting the

questions respecting polygamy and plural wives, as we felt we ought to do.

Question.—Who performed the marriage ceremony for Joseph Smith and Emma Hale? When? Where?

Answer.—I was married at South Bainbridge, New York; at the house of Squire Tarbell, by him, when I was in my 22d, or 23d year.

We here suggested that Mother Smith's History gave the date of the marriage as January 18th, 1827. To this she replied:

I think the date correct. My certificate of marriage was lost many years ago, in some of the marches we were forced to make.

In answer to a suggestion by us that she might mistake about who married father and herself; and that it was rumored that it was Sidney Rigdon, or a Presbyterian clergyman, she stated:

It was not Sidney Rigdon, for I did not see him for years after that. It was not a Presbyterian clergyman. I was visiting at Mr. [Josiah] Stowell's, who lived in Bainbridge, and saw your father there. I had no intention of marrying when I left home; but, during my visit at Mr. Stowell's, your father visited me there. My folks were bitterly opposed to him; and, being importuned by your father, aided by Mr. Stowell, who urged me to marry [Joseph], and preferring to marry him to any other man I knew, I consented. We went to Squire Tarbell's and were married. Afterwards, when father found that I was married, he sent for us. The account in Mother Smith's History is substantially correct as to date and place. Your father bought your uncle

Jesse's [Hale] place, off father's farm, and we lived there till the Book of Mormon was translated; and I think published. I was not in Palmyra long.

Q. How many children did you lose, mother, before I was born?

A. There were three. I buried one in Pennsylvania and a pair of twins in Ohio.

Q. Who were the twins that died?

A. They were not named.

Q. Who were the twins whom you took to raise?

A. I lost twins. Mrs. [Julia] Murdock had twins and died. Bro. [John] Murdock came to me and asked me to take them, and I took the babes [Julia and Joseph]. Joseph died at eleven months. They were both sick when your father was mobbed. The mob who tarred and feathered him, left the door open when they went out with him, the child relapsed and died. Julia lived, though weaker than the boy.

Q. When did you first know Sidney Rigdon? Where?

A. I was residing at father [Peter] Whitmer's, when I first saw Sidney Rigdon. I think he came there.

Q. Was this before or after the publication of the Book of Mormon?

A. The Book of Mormon had been translated and published some time before. Parley P. Pratt had united with the Church before I knew Sidney Rigdon, or heard of him. At the time the Book of Mormon was translated there was no church organized, Rigdon did not become acquainted with

Joseph and me till after the Church was established in 1830. How long after that I do not know, but it was some time.

Q. Who were scribes for father when translating the Book of Mormon?

A. Myself, Oliver Cowdery, Martin Harris, and my brother, Reuben Hale.

Q. Was Alva Hale?

A. I think not. He may have written some; but if he did, I do not remember it.

Q. What about the revelation on Polygamy? Did Joseph Smith have anything like it? What of spiritual wifery?

A. There was no revelation on either polygamy, or spiritual wives. There were some rumors of something of the sort, of which I asked my husband. He assured me that all there was of it was, that, in a chat about plural wives, he had said, "Well, such a system might possibly be, if everybody was agreed to it, and would behave as they should; but they would not; and, besides, it was contrary to the will of heaven."

No such thing as polygamy, or spiritual wifery, was taught, publically or privately, before my husband's death, that I have now, or ever had any knowledge of.

Q. Did he not have other wives than yourself?

A. He had no other wife but me; nor did he to my knowledge ever have.

Q. Did he not hold marital relation with women other than yourself?

A. He did not have improper relations with any woman that ever came to my knowledge.

Q. Was there nothing about spiritual wives that you recollect?

A. At one time my husband came to me and asked me if I had heard certain rumors about spiritual marriages, or anything of the kind; and assured me that if I had, that they were without foundation; that there was no such doctrine, and never should be with his knowledge, or consent. I know that he had no other wife or wives than myself, in any sense, either spiritual or otherwise.

Q. What is the truth of Mormonism?

A. I know Mormonism to be the truth; and believe the Church to have been established by divine direction. I have complete faith in it. In writing for your father I frequently wrote day after day, often sitting at the table close by him, he sitting with his face buried in his hat, with the stone in it, and dictating hour after hour with nothing between us.

Q. Had he not a book or manuscript from which he read, or dictated to you?

A. He had neither manuscript nor book to read from.

Q. Could he not have had, and you not [k]now it?

A. If he had anything of the kind he could not have concealed it from me.

Q. Are you sure that he had the plates at the time you were writing for him?

A. The plates often lay on the table without any attempt at concealment, wrapped in a small linen table cloth, which I had given him to fold them in. I once felt of the plates, as they thus lay on the table, tracing their outline and shape. They seemed to be pliable like thick paper, and would rustle with a metallic sound when the edges were moved by the thumb, as one does sometimes thumb the edges of a book.

Q. Where did father and Oliver Cowdery write?

A. Oliver Cowdery and your father wrote in the room where I was at work.

Q. Could not father have dictated the Book of Mormon to you, Oliver Cowdery and the others who wrote for him, after having first written it, or having first read it out of some book?

A. Joseph Smith [and for the first time she used his name direct, having usually used the words, "your father," or "my husband"] could neither write or dictate a coherent and well-worded letter; let alone dictating a book like the Book of Mormon. And, though I was an active participant in the scenes that transpired, and was present during the translation of the plates, and had cognizance of things as they transpired, it is marvelous to me, "a marvel and a wonder," as much so as to any one else.

Q. I should suppose that you would have uncovered the plates and examined them?

A. I did not attempt to handle the plates, other than I have told you, nor uncover them to look at them. I was satisfied that it was the work of God, and therefore did not feel it to be necessary to do so.

Major Bidamon here suggested: Did Mr. Smith forbid your examining the plates?

A. I do not think he did. I knew that he had

them, and was not specially curious about them. I moved them from place to place on the table, as it was necessary in doing my work.

Q. Mother, what is your belief about the authenticity, or origin of the Book of Mormon?

A. My belief is that the Book of Mormon is of divine authenticity—I have not the slightest doubt of it. I am satisfied that no man could have dictated the writing of the manuscripts unless he was inspired; for, when acting as his scribe, your father would dictate to me hour after hour; and when returning after meals, or after interruptions, he would at once begin where he had left off, without either seeing the manuscript or having any portion of it read to him. This was a usual thing for him to do. It would have been improbable that a learned man could do this; and, for one so ignorant and unlearned as he was, it was simply impossible.

Q. What was the condition of feeling between you and father?

A. It was good.

Q. Were you in the habit of quarreling?

A. No. There was no necessity for any quarreling. He knew that I wished for nothing but what was right; and, as he wished for nothing else, we did not disagree. He usually gave some heed to what I had to say. It was quite a grievous thing to many that I had any influence with him.

Q. What do you think of David Whitmer?

A. David Whitmer I believe to be a honest and truthful man. I think what he states may be relied on.

Q. It has been stated sometimes that you apostatized at father's death, and joined the Methodist Church. What do you say to this?

A. I have been called apostate; but I have never apostatized, nor forsaken the faith I at first accepted; but was called so because I would not accept their new fangled notion.

Q. By whom were you baptized? Do you remember?

A. I think by Oliver Cowdery, at Bainbridge.

Q. You say that you were married at South Bainbridge, and have used the word Bainbridge. Were they one and the same town?

A. No. There was Bainbridge and South Bainbridge; some distance apart; how far I don't know. I was in South Bainbridge.

These questions, and the answers she had given to them, were read to my mother by me, the day before my leaving Nauvoo for home, and were affirmed by her. Major Bidamon stated that he had frequently conversed with her on the subject of the translation of the Book of Mormon, and her present answers were substantially what she had always stated in regard to it.[151]

Did Emma suffer from any health problems?

In summer 1872, Emma fell down the cellar stairs in the Mansion House and, in so doing, fractured her left arm. Her accident was reported in the *Deseret News* on August 9, 1872: "Emma had her arm in a sling, having fallen down the cellar quite recently and broken her left arm just above the wrist, which she said was doing well."[152] Other than the fracture, Emma's health was not compromised.

Did Emma speak of Joseph in her final moments?

Photograph of Emma Smith.

On the evening of April 29, 1879, Emma's children rallied to her bedside. At the time, she did not recognize anyone. Her son Alexander wrote, "We are simply waiting the end, and it seems to be near, only God knows how near. I think sometimes I have passed through the worst, yet I know how hard it will be to give mother up." As the family waited, Alexander heard his mother call, "Joseph, Joseph:"[153]

I thought she meant my brother. He was in the room, and I spoke to him, and said, Joseph, mother wants you. I was at the head of the bed. My mother raised right up, lifted her left hand as high as she could raise it, and called, Joseph, I put my left arm under her shoulders, took her hand in mine, saying, Mother, what is it, laid her hand on her bosom, and she was dead; she had passed away.[154]

Emma Smith died at 4:20 a.m. on April 30, 1879, in Nauvoo at the age of seventy-four.

On May 2, 1879, a funeral service was held. Following the funeral, Emma was buried next to the remains of Joseph Smith in the Smith family graveyard near her home in Nauvoo.[155] A description of her burial clothes was given by Audentia Anderson to Vesta Crawford: "[Emma] was buried in a rather dark dress of plum or magenta shade, brocaded with flowers and leaves in a raised design."[156]

Were public announcements made of her death?

Joseph Smith III made the first public announcement in the RLDS periodical, the *Saints' Herald*: "On Friday, May 2d, neighbors, friends and relatives, bore [Emma's] remains to the place where our relations lie, and there we left them, where on her grave the gentle dew and genial sunshine, the storm and the calm, shall bless her repose until with them that sleep she shall rise to the eternal newness of everlasting life."[157]

Joseph A. Crawford, in "A Poem to Alexander H. Smith Upon the Passing of His Mother," which also appeared in the *Saints' Herald*, made the second public announcement:

> Weep not brother, no despairing,
> Grieving now should rend thy Breast;
> Out beyond the night of sorrow,
> Dawns a beautiful to-morrow;
> While through the rifted clouds appearing,
> Breaks the morn of endless rest;
> That awaits thy darling mother,
> Passed to Paradise, before,
> Where no pain or trouble, brother,
> E're will cross her pathway more.
> Now that she is calmly sleeping,
> 'Mid the darkling silent gloom,
> Waiting for the resurrection,
> Where the mortal gains perfection;
> Still thy sorrow, cease thy weeping,
> For the passage through the tomb,
> Dark and silent, brings awaking,
> To a life eternal, bright;
> For the day-dawn grandly breaking,
> Wafts to her celestial light.

Grand has been her mission. Living
When the gospel sun-burst come;
Side by side with Joseph bearing
Up the standard. Gladly sharing
All the trials; calmly Giving
For the gospel, friends and home.
Pressing onward, faltering never;
Though thy father in the strife.
Died a martyr, crossed deaths river,
To the golden port of life.

Then she saw the gospel standard,
Overthrown by Satan's might;
Though the darkness closed around her,
Error's bondage never bound her;
When the ship of Zion wandered,
Out of darkness, into night.
Ever trusting that high heaven,
Would the trusty pilot call;
By whose hands, the bands all riven,
From the shackled helm should fall.

God be praised, thy aged mother
Did not pass behind the veil;
"Till she heard the proclamation,
Ushering in the restoration."[158]

On May 21, 1879, the *Deseret News* in Salt Lake City published an article about her passing. The article recalled that "to old members of this Church the deceased was well known, as a lady of more than ordinary intelligence and force of character." The remainder of the article was not complimentary toward Emma.[159]

A notice in the *Woman's Exponent* on May 15, 1879, viewed Emma's life in more favorable terms:

> Mrs. Emma Bidamon, died in Nauvoo on the 30th of April. Among the Latter-day Saints, in days gone by, she was familiarly known as "Sister Emma," wife of the Prophet Joseph Smith. She was considered rather a remarkable woman, possessing great influence and unusually strong characteristics, which if properly directed, as in the early days of this Church, would have made her name illustrious in the history of the women of the Latter-day Saints down to the end of time.[160]

Conclusion

So much of Emma's life is cloaked in silence. Perhaps the silence was by choice. From what has been preserved in the collected memory of others, there is much in Emma's life to celebrate.

- To Joseph Smith, she was "My beloved Emma—she that was my wife, even the wife of my youth, and the choice of my heart. . . undaunted, firm, and unwavering—unchangeable, affectionate Emma!"[161]
- She was the first to learn that Joseph had received the gold plates from the angel Moroni.
- She was a scribe to the Book of Mormon translation and said of that work: "The Book of Mormon is of divine authenticity—I have not the slightest doubt of it."[162]
- Her testimony of the Book of Mormon and the prophetic calling of Joseph Smith led to her baptism on June 28, 1830.
- A month after entering baptismal waters, Joseph received an important revelation from the Lord for Emma. In the revelation, Emma was told, "Behold, thy sins are forgiven thee, and thou art an elect lady, whom I have called" (D&C 25:3). The revelation is personal for Emma, yet latter-day prophets have used it as counsel for other women.

- Emma became an exemplar to others of the faith. Mother Smith wrote, "If elders were sent away to preach, she was the first to volunteer her services to assist in clothing them for their journey. Whatever her own privations, she scorned to complain."[163]
- She bore nine children, raising the five who lived to adulthood.
- She compiled two hymnals for the LDS Church and one for the RLDS Church. These songs of praise speak volumes of her love for the Lord and for her knowledge that "the song of the righteous is a prayer unto me" (D&C 25:12).
- With two babies in her arms and two children at her skirts, Emma walked across the frozen Mississippi carrying Joseph Smith's papers, including the new translation of the Bible.
- She graciously welcomed both the poor and the acclaimed into her home.
- She was president of the Female Relief Society of Nauvoo. Under her guidance, the women of her society searched for those in need and ministered to them. Through their service heavy burdens were lifted, sorrows too severe to be carried alone were shared, and necessities needed to sustain life were freely proffered. Her society today numbers in the millions and has proven a charitable force for good throughout the world.
- Emma participated in temple ordinance work, including acting as proxy for extended family members. She also was sealed to Joseph Smith for time and eternity.
- She wrote letters in defense of Joseph Smith to the governor of Illinois, even traveling to Quincy to meet with him on this important matter.

- She cared for Lucy Mack Smith, her mother-in-law, for five years, during which time Lucy suffered from crippling arthritis.
- Emma maintained and preserved properties in Nauvoo that were significant to the life of Joseph Smith and the Latter-day Saints.
- She was a caring mother to her own children and those of others.
- In her seventy-fourth year, in speaking of Joseph's prophetic calling, she said, "I believe he was everything he professed to be."[164]

What do you think of Emma Smith? Joseph loved her. Emmeline B. Wells thought "Emma was a great solace to her husband in all his persecutions and the severe ordeals through which he passed; she was always ready to encourage and comfort him, devoted to his interests, and was constantly by him whenever it was possible."[165] Joseph Smith Sr., in a patriarchal blessing given to Emma, pronounced, "The holy angels shall watch over thee: and thou shalt be saved in the kingdom of God even so, Amen."[166]

Notes

1. Joseph Smith Jr., *History of the Church of Jesus Christ of Latter-day Saints* (Salt Lake City: Deseret Book, 1980), 4:548.

2. Smith, *History of the Church*, 5:21.

3. Smith, *History of the Church*, 5:21.

4. Smith, *History of the Church*, 5:25.

5. Smith, *History of the Church*, 5:92.

6. Emma Smith McCallum's Reminiscences, as quoted in Buddy Youngreen, *Reflections of Emma, Joseph Smith's Wife* (Provo, Utah: Maasai, Inc., 1982), 61.

7. Emmeline B. Wells, "L.D.S. Women of the Past. Personal Impressions," *Woman's Exponent* 36, no. 7 (February 1908): 490.

8. Scot Facer Proctor and Maurine Jensen Proctor, eds., *History of Joseph Smith by His Mother: Revised and Enhanced* (Salt Lake City: Bookcraft, 1996), 128, fn. 10.

9. Inez A. Kennedy, *Recollections of the Pioneers of Lee County* (Dixon, Ill.: n.p., 1893), 96.

10. Lucy Mack Smith, *Biographical Sketches of Joseph Smith the Prophet, and his Progenitors for many Generations* (London: S. W. Richards, 1853 [reprint London: William Bowden, 1969]), 103; See also Compiled Material on Susquehanna County, Pennsylvania, 1887–1963, Church History Library, The Church of Jesus Christ of Latter-day Saints, Salt Lake City, Utah.

11. Joseph Smith—History 1:56.

12. Smith, *Biographical Sketches,* 104.

13. Statement of Isaac Hale, Affirmed to and subscribed before Chas. Dimon, J. P., March 20, 1834, as reprinted in Emily C. Blackman, *History of Susquehanna County, Pennsylvania* (Baltimore, Md.: Regional Publishing Company, 1980), 578.

14. Smith, *History of the Church,* 1:17.

15. Statement of Isaac Hale, reprinted in Blackman, *History of Susquehanna County, Pennsylvania,* 578; See also Roy Arthur Cheville, *Joseph and Emma Smith, Companions for Seventeen and a Half Years, 1827–1844* (Independence, MO.: Herald Publishing House, 1977).

16. Joseph Knight, quoted in William G. Hartley "The Knight Family: Ever Faithful to the Prophet," *Ensign* 19, no. 1 (January 1989): 44.

17. Proctor and Proctor, *Revised and Enhanced History,* 126.

18. Smith, *Biographical Sketches,* 105.

19. Joseph Smith III, "Last Testimony of Sister Emma," *Saints' Herald* 26, no. 19 (October 1, 1879): 289, col. 2.

20. Statement of Isaac Hale, as quoted in Howe, *Mormonism Unvailed: or, A Faithful Account of that Singular Imposition and Delusion, from its Rise to the Present Time. With Sketches of the Characters of Its Propagators, and a full detail of the Manner in which the Famous Golden Bible was Brought before the World. To which are Added, Inquiries into the Probability that the Historical Part of the Said Bible was Written by One Solomon Spalding, More than Twenty Years Ago, and by Him Intended to Have been Published as a Romance* (Painesville, Ohio: E. B. Howe, 1834), 234.

21. Smith, *History of the Church,* 1:17.

22. Proctor and Proctor, *Revised and Enhanced History,* 129.

23. Proctor and Proctor, *Revised and Enhanced History,* 248–49.

24. Joseph Smith—History 1:59.

25. Joseph Smith—History 1:61–62.

26. *The Susquehanna Register*, [Montrose] May 1, 1834, as cited in Porter, "A Study of the Origins of The Church of Jesus Christ of Latter-day Saints in the States of New York and Pennsylvania, 1816–1831," (Ph.D. dissertation, Brigham Young University, 1971), 133.

27. *The Susquehanna Register*, [Montrose] May 1, 1834, as cited in Porter, "A Study of the Origins," 133.

28. Nels Madsen, "Visit to Emma Smith Bidemon [*sic*] 1931," Church History Library.

29. Smith, "Last Testimony of Sister Emma," *Saints' Herald* 26, no. 19 (October 1, 1879): 290, col. 1.

30. Proctor and Proctor, *Revised and Enhanced History*, 161.

31. Proctor and Proctor, *Revised and Enhanced History*, 176.

32. Proctor and Proctor, *Revised and Enhanced History*, 184.

33. Smith, "Last Testimony of Sister Emma," *Saints' Herald* 26, no. 19 (October 1, 1879): 290, col. 1.

34. Reuben Miller, October 21, 1848, Church History Library. See also Richard L. Anderson, "Reuben Miller, Recorder of Oliver Cowdery's Reaffirmations," *BYU Studies* 8, no. 3 (Spring 1968): 278.

35. E. C. Briggs, "Brother Joseph Smith," *Saints' Herald* 31, no. 25 (June 4, 1884): 397.

36. William H. Kelley and G. A. Blakeslee, "Letter from Elder W. H. Kelley, 15 January 1882, Richmond, Missouri," *Saints' Herald* 29, no. 5 (March 1, 1882): 68.

37. Smith, *History of the Church*, 4:555.

38. Smith, *History of the Church*, 4:552–53.

39. Wells, "L.D.S. Women of the Past," *Woman's Exponent* 36, no. 7 (February 1908): 490.

40. Smith, *History of the Church*, 4:606–7.

41. Smith, *History of the Church*, 2:273.

42. Hymnal, 1835 Facsimile 5, Church History Library.

43. William Holmes Walker, *The Life Incidents and Travels of Elder William Holmes Walker and his Association with Joseph Smith, the Prophet* (n.p.: Elizabeth Jane Walker Piepgrass, 1943), 8.

44. Bruce R. McConkie, *Mormon Doctrine* 2d ed. (Salt Lake City: Bookcraft, 1979), 217.

45. Proctor and Proctor, *Revised and Enhanced History*, 305–6.

46. Smith, *Biographical Sketches*, 204.

47. Albert G. Riddle, *History of Geauga and Lake Counties, Ohio* (Philadelphia: Williams Brothers, 1878), 248.

48. Proctor and Proctor, *Revised and Enhanced History*, 306.

49. Smith, *History of the Church*, 1:261–62.

50. Smith, *History of the Church*, 6:316.

51. Smith, *History of the Church*, 5:362.

52. Alexander Hale Smith, sermon given July 1, 1903, Bottlineau, North Dakota, as quoted in Gracia N. Jones, "My Great-Great-Grandmother, Emma Hale Smith," *Ensign* 22, no. 18 (August 1992): 38.

53. Joseph Smith to Emma Smith, June 6, 1832, as quoted in Dean C. Jessee, ed., *The Personal Writings of Joseph Smith* (Salt Lake City: Deseret Book, 1984), 237–38.

54. Patriarchal Blessing given to Emma Smith by Joseph Smith Sr., December 9, 1834, Kirtland, Ohio, as transcribed by Oliver Cowdery. Patriarchal Blessing Book 2:7, Church History Library.

55. Joseph Smith to Emma Smith, October 13, 1832, as quoted in Jessee, *Personal Writings of Joseph Smith*, 252–53.

56. Joseph Smith to Emma Smith, May 18, 1834, Church History Library.

57. Joseph Smith to Emma Smith, June 4, 1834, as quoted in Jessee, *Personal Writings of Joseph Smith*, 323–25.

58. Joseph Smith to Emma Smith, November 4, 1838, Church History Library.

59. Joseph Smith to Emma Smith, November 12, 1838, Church History Library.

60. Joseph Smith to Emma Smith, December 1, 1838, Church History Library.

61. Joseph Smith to Emma Smith, March 21, 1839, as quoted in Jessee, *Personal Writings of Joseph Smith*, 408–09.

62. Joseph Smith to Emma Smith, April 4, 1839, as quoted in Jessee, *Personal Writings of Joseph Smith*, 425–27.

63. Statement of Joseph Smith III, quoted in Mary Audentia Smith Anderson and Bertha Ardentia Anderson Hulmes, eds., *Joseph III and the Restoration* (Independence, MO.: Herald Publishing House, 1952), 2.

64. Emma Smith to Joseph Smith, March 21, 1839, as quoted in Jessee, *Personal Writings of Joseph Smith*, 388–89.

65. Smith, *History of the Church*, 4:337. See also R. B. Thompson, clerk, "Report of the First Presidency," *Times and Seasons* 2, no. 12 (April 15, 1841): 385.

66. Smith, *History of the Church*, 2:353.

67. Smith, *History of the Church*, 4:370.

68. Wilford Woodruff Journals and Papers 1828–1898, March 16, 1839, Church History Library. See also Wilford Woodruff Collection, 1831–1898, Church History Library.

69. Smith, *History of the Church*, 7:260.

70. Statement of John Bernhisel, in L. John Nuttall, "Diary One," September 10, 1879, 335, L. Tom Perry Special Collections, Brigham Young University, Provo, Utah.

71. Edmund C. Briggs, "A Visit to Nauvoo in 1856," *Journal of History* 9, no. 4 (October 1916): 453.

72. Emma Smith Bidamon to Joseph Smith III, December

2, 1867; Emma Hale Smith Letters, 1866–1871, Church History Library.

73. Smith, *History of the Church*, 3:375.

74. Wilford Woodruff, Journal, May 1839, as cited in Matthias Cowley, *Wilford Woodruff, History of His Life and Labors* (Salt Lake City: Bookcraft, 1964), 104. See also Wilford Woodruff, Journals and Papers 1828–1898, Church History Library.

75. Proctor and Proctor, *Revised and Enhanced History*, 447, 449.

76. Proctor and Proctor, *Revised and Enhanced History*, 424.

77. Joseph Smith to Emma Smith, November 9, 1839, Church History Library.

78. Joseph Smith to Emma Smith, January 20, 1840, as quoted in Jessee, *Personal Writings of Joseph Smith*, 454.

79. Hyrum L. Andrus and Helen Mae Andrus, *They Knew the Prophet* (Salt Lake City: Deseret Book, 1999), 164.

80. Smith, *History of the Church*, 4:16.

81. Smith, *History of the Church*, 6:165–66; See also Gracia Lorena Normandeau Jones, *Priceless Gifts: Celebrating the Holidays with Joseph and Emma* (American Fork, Utah: Covenant Communications, 1998).

82. Wells, "L.D.S. Women of the Past," *Woman's Exponent* 36, no. 7 (February 1908): 490.

83. Smith, *History of the Church*, 4:17–18.

84. Susan Easton Black, Harvey B. Black, and Brandon Plewe, *Property Transactions in Nauvoo, Hancock County, Illinois and Surrounding Communities (1839–1859)* 7 vols. (Wilmington, Delaware: World Vital Records, Inc., 2006), 6:3643–51.

85. Autobiography of Harvey Cluff [typescript], 4–5. Perry Special Collections.

86. Autobiography of Luman Shurtliff [typescript], 52–53. Perry Special Collections.

87. Kimball, "Auto-biography," *Woman's Exponet* 12, no. 7 (September 1, 1883): 51.

88. Kimball, "Auto-biography," *Woman's Exponet* 12, no. 7 (September 1, 1883): 51.

89. See Smith, *History of the Church*, 4:552.

90. Relief Society Minute Book, March 1842–March 1844, March 17, 1842, Church History Library.

91. E. R. Snow, "The Female Relief Society of Nauvoo— What is it?" *Times and Seasons* 3, no. 17 (July 1, 1842): 846.

92. Joseph Smith, "To the Saints of God," *Times and Seasons* 3, no. 24 (October 15, 1842): 952.

93. Smith, *History of the Church*, 4:606.

94. Relief Society Minute Book, March 1842–March 1844, March 17, 1842, Church History Library.

95. Joseph Fielding Smith, comp., *Teachings of the Prophet Joseph Smith* (Salt Lake City: Deseret Book, 1961), 228–29.

96. Relief Society Minute Book, March 1842–March 1844, March 17, 1842, Church History Library.

97. Jill Mulvay Derr, Janath Russell Cannon, and Maureen Ursenbach Beecher, *Women of Covenant: The Story of Relief Society* (Salt Lake City: Deseret Book, 1992), 31.

98. Relief Society Minute Book, March 1842–March 1844, May 27, 1842, Church History Library.

99. Derr, Cannon, and Beecher, *Women of Covenant*, 33–34.

100. Relief Society Minute Book, March 1842–March 1844, April 19, 1842, Church History Library.

101. Smith, *Teachings of the Prophet Joseph Smith*, 259.

102. Maureen Ursenbach Beecher, "Eliza R. Snow's Nauvoo Journal," *BYU Studies* 15, no. 4 (Summer 1975): 400– 401.

103. Relief Society Minute Book, March 1842–March 1844, March 24, 1842, Church History Library.

104. Wells, "L.D.S. Women of the Past," *Woman's Exponent* 36, no. 7 (February 1908): 490.

105. Smith, *History of the Church*, 5:166.

106. Smith, *History of the Church*, 5:167–168.

107. "Recollections of the Prophet Joseph Smith," *Juvenile Instructor* 27 (July 1, 1892): 399.

108. Smith, *History of the Church*, 5:107.

109. Smith, *History of the Church*, 5:115–17.

110. Smith, *History of the Church*, 5:118.

111. Smith, *History of the Church*, 5:134.

112. Nauvoo Baptismal Records of the Dead, Book A 45, 143, Book C 153. See also Susan Easton Black and Harvey Bischoff Black, *Annotated Record of Baptisms for the Dead, 1840–1845, Nauvoo, Hancock County, Illinois* 7 vols. (Provo, Utah: The Center for Family History and Genealogy, Brigham Young University, 2002), 6: 3354–56.

113. Joseph Smith to Emma Smith, June 23, 1844, Church History Library.

114. Smith, *History of the Church*, 6:549.

115. Benjamin F. Johnson, *My Life's Review* (Heber City, Utah: Archive Publishers, 2001), 120.

116. Smith, *History of the Church*, 6:549, 555.

117. Joseph Smith to Emma Smith, June 25, 1844, as quoted in Jessee, *Personal Writings of Joseph Smith*, 603–4.

118. Joseph Smith to Emma Smith, June 27, 1844, Church History Library.

119. Smith, *History of the Church*, 6:621–22.

120. Smith, *History of the Church*, 6:627.

121. B. W. Richmond, "The Prophet's Death!" *Deseret Evening News* 9, no. 5 (November 27, 1875): 3.

122. Eliza R. Snow, "The Assassination of Gen'ls Joseph Smith and Hyrum Smith, First Presidents of the Church of Latter Day Saints: who were massacred by a Mob, in Carthage, Hancock County, Ill, on the 27th June 1844," *Times and Seasons* 5, no. 12 (July 1, 1844): 575.

123. See Anderson and Hulmes, *Joseph Smith III and the Restoration*, 85.

124. Eliza R. Snow, "Lines written on the birth of an infant son of Mrs. Emma, widow of the late General Joseph Smith," *Times and Seasons* 5, no. 22 (December 1, 1844): 735.

125. John M. Bernhisel to Emma Smith, October 9, 1847, John Milton Bernhisel Collection, 1829–1894, John Milton Bernhisel, Papers 1818–1872, Church History Library.

126. Madsen, "Visit to Mrs. Emma Smith Bidemon [*sic*] 1931," Church History Library.

127. Emma Smith, "To the Editor of the *New York Sun*," *Times and Seasons* 6, no. 21 (January 20, 1846): 1096.

128. *Joseph Smith III Memoirs*, 50, as quoted in Murdock, *Joseph and Emma's Julia*, 80.

129. Thomas L. Kane, *The Mormons: A Discourse Delivered before The Historical Society of Pennsylvania: March 26, 1850* (Philadelphia, Pa.: King & Baird, 1850), 4.

130. Statement of Charles Lanman, quoted in E. Cecil McGavin, *The Nauvoo Temple* (Salt Lake City: Deseret Book, 1962), 121.

131. *Joseph Smith III Memoirs*, 45, as quoted in Murdock, *Joseph and Emma's Julia*, 80.

132. Vesta Pierce Crawford, Notes on Emma Smith, n.d., Church History Library.

133. Sarah Melissa Granger Kimball to Marinda Hyde, January 2, 1848, Church History Library.

134. See Bidamon Family Papers, 1836–1964, Church History Library.

135. Emma Smith Bidamon to Lewis Bidamon, April 20, 1850, in Bidamon Family Papers, 1836–1964, Church History Library.

136. Charles E. Bidamon to Warren L. Van Dine, September 9, 1940, as cited in Youngreen, *Reflections of Emma*, 84–85, fn. 44. See also Charles E. Bidamon to L. L. Hudson, August 10, 1940, Church History Library.

137.   Briggs, "A Visit to Nauvoo in 1856," *Journal of History* 9, no. 4 (October 1916): 453.

138.   Diary of David Hyrum Smith, February 17, 1862, as quoted in Youngreen, *Reflections of Emma*, 83. See also Erwin Paul Youngreen Collection 1840–1938, Church History Library.

139.   Joseph Smith to William Smith, December 18, 1835, as quoted in Smith, *History of the Church*, 2:342.

140.   See "Julia Murdock Smith Middleton" [ca. 1840s], Church History Library. See also S. Reed Murdock, *Joseph and Emma's Julia: the "Other" Twin* (Salt Lake City: Eborn Books, 2004).

141.   See Roger D. Launius, *Father Figure: Joseph Smith III and the Creation of the Reorganized Church* (Independence, MO.: Herald Publishing House, 1990).

142.   See Valeen Tippetts Avery, *From Mission to Madness: Last Son of the Mormon Prophet* (Urbana and Chicago: University of Illinois Press, 1998).

143.   Orson Pratt, "Celestial Marriage," *Journal of Discourses*, 13:194.

144.   Brigham Young, "Increase of Saints since Joseph Smith's death—Joseph Smith's sons . . . ," *Journal of Discourses*, 15:136.

145.   Frederick Piercy, as quoted in James Lindforth, ed., *Route from Liverpool to Great Salt Lake Valley* (Liverpool: Franklin D. Richards, 1855), 65–66.

146.   Letter of Joseph Fielding Smith written to Levira Smith on 28 June 1860. Church History Library.

147.   *The History of the Reorganized Church of Jesus Christ of Latter Day Saints,* 5 vols. (Independence, MO.: Herald House, 1967), 3:352.

148.   Brigham Young, "The United Order is the Order of the Kingdom where God and Christ Dwell," *Journal of Discourses*, 17:159.

149.   Wilford Woodruff, "Liberty of Conscience," *Journal of Discourses*, 23:131.

150. Madsen, "Visit to Mrs. Emma Smith Bidemon [*sic*] 1931," Church History Library.

151. Smith, "Last Testimony of Sister Emma," *Saints' Herald* 26, no. 19 (October 1, 1879): 290, col. 1.

152. *Deseret Evening News* 5, no. 222 (August 9, 1872).

153. Alexander Smith to Lizzie Smith, April 28–29, 1879, as quoted in Vesta Pierce Crawford, Notes on Emma Smith, n.d., Church History Library.

154. See Alexander H. Smith, "Sermon by Alexander H. Smith, at Bottineau, N. D., July 1, 1903," *Zion's Ensign* 14, no. 53 (July 1, 1903): 7.

155. See Burial place and Tomb of Mrs. Emma Bidamon [ca. 1900]. See also Albert L. Childers, "An Account of the Reinterment of the Remains of Joseph Smith, Hyrum Smith and Emma Smith . . . 1958," Church History Library.

156. Vesta Pierce Crawford, Notes on Emma Smith, n.d., Church History Library.

157. Joseph Smith III, "Editorial Items," *Saints' Herald* 26, no. 10 (May 15, 1879): 152.

158. Joseph A. Crawford, "To Brother Alexander H. Smith," *Saints' Herald* 26, no. 15 (June 1879): 180.

159. "Death of Emma Smith," *Deseret News* 28, no. 16 (May 21, 1879): 243, col. 2.

160. "Home Affairs," *Woman's Exponent* 7, no. 24 (May 15, 1879): 243, col. 2.

161. Smith, *History of the Church*, 5:107.

162. Madsen, "Visit to Mrs. Emma Smith Bidemon [*sic*] 1931," Church History Library.

163. Proctor and Proctor, *Revised and Enhanced History*, 305–6.

164. Nels Madsen, "Visit to Emma Smith Bidemon [*sic*] 1931," Church History Library.

165. Wells, "L.D.S. Women of the Past," *Woman's Exponent* 36, no. 7 (February 1908): 490.

166. Patriarchal Blessing given to Emma Smith by Joseph

Smith Sr., December 9, 1834, Kirtland, Ohio, as
transcribed by Oliver Cowdery. Patriarchal Blessing
Book 2:7, Church History Library.

Author Biographical Information

Susan Easton Black is a Professor of Church History and Doctrine at Brigham Young University. She is a former Associate Dean of General Education and Honors and an Eliza R. Snow Fellow. Professor Black is the recipient of many academic awards, including the Karl G. Maeser Distinguished Faculty Lecturer Award, the first female faculty member at BYU to be so honored. She has written over 100 books and 250 articles.

SETTING THE RECORD STRAIGHT SERIES

MORMONS & MASONS

GILBERT W. SCHARFFS, Ph.D.

MORMONS POLYGAMY

JESSIE L. EMBRY

BLACKS & THE MORMON PRIESTHOOD

MARCUS H. MARTINS, Ph.D.

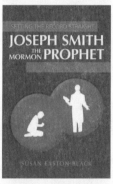

JOSEPH SMITH THE MORMON PROPHET

SUSAN EASTON BLACK

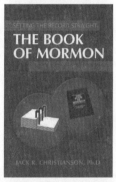

THE BOOK OF MORMON

JACK R. CHRISTIANSON, Ph.D.

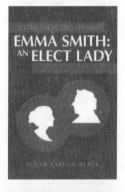

EMMA SMITH: AN ELECT LADY

SUSAN EASTON BLACK

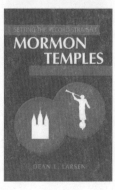

MORMON TEMPLES

DEAN L. LARSEN

THE WORD OF WISDOM

STEVEN C. HARPER, Ph.D.

JOSEPH SMITH: PRESIDENTIAL CANDIDATE

ARNOLD K. GARR, Ph.D.